BETTER THE SECOND TIME

How to Have an Amazing Second Marriage

By Chris and Denise Widener

Made for Success
PUBLISHING

Made for Success Publishing
P.O. Box 1775 Issaquah, WA 98027
www.MadeForSuccessPublishing.com

Distributed by Made for Success Publishing

First Printing

Library of Congress Cataloging-in-Publication data

Widener, Chris and Denise
Better the Second Time: How to Have
an Amazing Second Marriage

p. cm.

ISBN: 978-1-64146-441-3 (PBK)
ISBN: 978-1-64146-446-8 (EBK)
ISBN: 978-1-64146-447-5 (audio)

Printed in the United States of America

For further information contact Made for Success Publishing
+14255266480 or email *service@madeforsuccess.net*

Contents

Our Story

Denise and my relationship started out like a lot of relationship stories begin nowadays, with a date arranged through an online dating service. Thankfully, Denise swiped right on me after I swiped right on her!

After chatting a bit, we decided to go on a date — lunch in Scottsdale. I walked in and saw her sitting at the bar in the restaurant, waiting for me to arrive. Denise is in corporate sales, so she was dressed *sharp*! I remember thinking "Wow!" I thought she was beautiful. *Very* put together.

I introduced myself, and we grabbed a table. We began to talk about online dating, our lives, and all the things you talk about on a first date. I really liked her.

Denise is a very healthy eater, which I found out right away, so I decided to go with the salad. I did, however, have crispy shrimp on the salad, which she said wasn't too bad for me. She even asked for a bite!

The date went well, we gave each other a quick hug and away we went.

This happened around the same time my son was in the beginning stages of his high-tech start-up. He was just about to get a significant venture investment, so I decided to move back to Seattle from Scottsdale to help him. Denise and I continued to chat, and I asked her to another lunch to tell her I was very interested in her but that I was moving halfway across the country.

We had another great date. We actually sat next to each other in the booth at that lunch. She mentioned that she was interested in me but didn't know how it would work with me in Seattle. She did have some friends in the Seattle area, so we thought maybe she could come and visit. Who knew? After lunch, I walked her to her car and we gave each other a nice peck on the lips. Nothing too sensual, just a peck. It was *nice*.

I moved a few days later. Denise then left for a three-week trip through Greece and Italy with some friends. I saw her Instagram posts and followed her trip. We didn't contact each other, though.

When Denise got back, we started to talk a bit on the phone and eventually it turned into every morning and night, seven days a week, for sometimes an hour or more. We didn't see each other for two months after meeting each other but spent probably 80+ hours on the phone. Frankly, I liked that. It gave us the chance to really get to know each other. We talked through a lot. Of course, we started with the basics, but as we got to know each other, the talks became deeper. I was in love with her before I ever saw her again after that second lunch.

We decided to take a trip to Las Vegas and see some shows and get to know each other. That went great and we had a lot of fun. A few weeks later she came up to Seattle for a long weekend, and we visited all the sites that you should see during the beautiful Seattle summers.

After this, I mentioned to Denise that I didn't think vacations were the best way to see if something is real. I mean, vacations are fun, but they aren't real life. I suggested that I come down and see her in Scottsdale. I suggested a week. She suggested two weeks, and I gladly took her up on it!

I found out that this was a big deal for Denise. She had been divorced for six years and had never allowed another man in her house while her two girls were there. I respected that and considered it a great honor that she trusted me that way. I had talked with the girls a few times on the phone over the previous months so I had some interaction with them. Denise asked them what they thought about me coming down for a couple of weeks and they were on board with it.

It was a great two weeks. Plenty of fun but also lots of "real-life." We even had our first disagreement and we got through it fine with lots of discussion. Our relationship was working.

I knew that I didn't want to do long distance. I wanted to be with Denise, so I decided to move back down to Scottsdale at the end of the summer to be with her and the girls.

We were engaged shortly thereafter, and soon after that, we were married in a beautiful intimate ceremony in Florence, Italy. The rest, as they say, is history!

Some might say, "That sounds quick." Well, frankly it was quick by some standards, but here is what we thought:

Some people who move quickly stay together their whole lives, and some people who date a long time get divorced. It isn't really about how long you date, but more in finding the right person, going into the relationship with your eyes open, having the right philosophies, the right strategies to make a marriage *amazing*, and making a commitment.

Better the Second Time is rooted in reality. It is what Denise and I believe and how we interact with each other to keep our relationship vibrant, loving and *amazing*. We began to work on and talk about these concepts shortly after we began dating and when we knew that we had something special. It is also rooted in research, both from the sources we will mention in the book as well as my work for 14 years as a pastor working with hundreds of couples before I began to write and speak full time. It is also rooted in experience. Between the two of us, Denise and I were married 37 years to our first spouses. We knew what worked and what didn't work. We knew what experience had taught us, both the good and the bad.

Denise and I are still learning. We are still growing. We are still firmly rooted in the idea that we are a *team*. We are bound together and seeking to have an amazing marriage. We hope that the thoughts that we share with you will challenge and encourage you. Challenge you to make the changes and have the conversations that you need to have. Encourage you to know that you *can* do it!

It is possible. There are many people out there who beat the odds and have amazing second marriages. We hope and pray that your marriage is one of them, and you live your lives together in joy and happiness no matter what life throws at you!

Introduction

Let's start with the bad news and get it right out of the way: The best research shows that 67% of second marriages fail.

But, as they say, you can make statistics say anything, and there are many variables that determine whether you succeed or fail in your second marriage. In spite of the seemingly negative statistics, you and your spouse can have a thriving — yes even *amazing* — relationship. In a moment, I will get to some of those variables.

Marriage is tough. It doesn't matter whether it is your first, second or even third. As I say in my speeches, you put two people, no matter how much they love each other, inside of a house for years and years and they are bound to hit some rough patches. Why? It's obvious, really. They are two different people. They have different personalities, needs, and desires, ways of going about doing things and many others. You and your fiancé or spouse are *different*. Couple that with the worst trait of human nature, selfishness, and you have a recipe for disaster.

Some people become overwhelmed and undone by their problems, while others overcome them. The difference between successful and unsuccessful marriages is not the absence of obstacles but the presence of perseverance. Not just "white-knuckle, I'm just going to stick it out" perseverance but *educated*, *disciplined*, and *focused* perseverance.

How you persevere through the ups and downs of your marriage makes all the difference. That is what this book is about: how to do it so you have an amazing marriage.

In order to get to an amazing marriage, you must start by eliminating the expectation that marriage will be easy. It isn't. It takes work. It takes lots of forgiveness and understanding. It requires that you view your spouse as a teammate, not the competition. What is good for him or her is good for you. What is bad for him or her is bad for you. There is no win-lose in marriage. There is only win-win or lose-lose. That's the way it works.

Now for the good news:

First, you don't have to be one of the 67%. You can be part of the 33%. That is a choice. It isn't like going to Vegas and throwing the dice and 67% of marriages fail by chance. It is choice, not chance. You can choose to be successful in your second marriage. Certainly, it helps if your spouse is on board with this philosophy. If he or she isn't, it is going to be tough. Amazing marriages take two people working together toward a common goal.

Amazing marriages take time. In fact, I worked at a bookstore when I was in college, and I have always remembered the title of a book we sold: *Good Marriages Take Time. Bad Marriages Take More Time.* Truth. It takes time. If you are willing to put in the time to grow and develop yourself and apply that growth in practical ways and your spouse is, too, you will have a great shot at an amazing marriage. The key is the application. It does no good to read, and even agree, that you shouldn't yell at your spouse, and then go off and yell at your spouse. Your learning must be practically applied, and there is no better laboratory than two people in a home.

Now, here is an interesting research finding: Most people think they worked at their failed marriage and their spouse didn't, or at least their spouse should have worked harder. Consider this research tidbit from Health Research Funding:

13% of women who have divorced said they wished that they had worked harder to save their marriage, but 65% of them say they wished their spouse had worked harder.

31% of men who have divorced say that they wished they'd worked harder to save their marriage, but 3 out of 4 men say their ex-wife should have done more.

Do you see that? Most people give themselves credit for working at it while not giving credit to their former spouse. Most people place the blame firmly on the backs of their former partner. When you're playing the blame game, it is less likely that you are taking a long, deep look in the mirror and learning lessons about what you contributed to the demise of your first marriage. Until we do that, it's difficult to address those issues so that they are rectified and you are healthy for your second marriage.

So, what are the other variables that determine your likelihood of having a successful second marriage? Some of the following are taken from the Marriage Foundation in Cambridge, while others are from Health Research Funding. Let's take a look at some of the key variables. As you read them, you will realize that some of them put you in a better place and increase your likelihood of having an amazing marriage if you meet the criteria or how you deal with it if you don't.

The first variable is the age of the couple. Simply put, the older you are, the more likely you are to succeed in your second marriage. This is probably explained because older people tend to be wiser, having learned from prior mistakes, they are more secure financially, and there are usually no longer children in the house. As the Marriage Foundation also points out, older couples tend to operate out of what is called the "commitment theory." That is, they usually have much more intentionality in their decisions.

The second variable is the income of the couple. Now, as with age, or any of these variables, this is no guarantee, and some people, whether rich or poor, old or young, will still get divorced, while others in that category will develop amazing marriages. It is a choice, remember? But these variables have attributes that make it harder to succeed. Not impossible, just harder. The research shows that an income of $50,000 a year or more increases the likelihood that you will make it in your second marriage.

Income is a variable because low income creates stress. I think we can all agree on that. When you get to the end of your month and see only $4 in your bank account and hundreds of dollars of bills piling up, that is stressful. And when we are stressed, it makes it more difficult not to get grumpy, and grumpiness leads to not getting along with others. Throw in some blame and guilt that you may put on your spouse for not making enough money or helping out financially and you have a setup for a breakdown of your marriage.

Do rich people get divorced? Yes, they do. But not because they have the stress of a low income. The higher your income, the less likely you will get divorced.

The third variable is education. The statistics show that 85% of those who have a bachelor's degree and get married for the second time will make it to their 10th anniversary. Again, noting that statistics don't always tell the whole story and that sometimes you have to dig in and read into them a bit, there may be a simple explanation for this. Is it because smarter people don't get divorced? Or is it that the degree is a magical "stay married" card? No. My guess would be that goes back to the other variable: People with college degrees make more money.

The case could also be made, or at least speculated about, that those who go on to pursue further education, as well as spend more time learning about how to have a better marriage, will stay happily married. It is unknown, but that would at least be a fair hypothesis.

It may also be generally true that those who have graduated may be goal-oriented and thus look at marriage in a different way than others in regard to achieving an amazing marriage.

The fourth variable is if children from a former marriage are in the home. Raising children is tough. Figuring out how to raise someone else's children is tougher. Throw in the possibility of a difficult-to-get-along-with former spouse, and it makes it even tougher. Learning to establish the right role for you as the stepparent is imperative in giving yourself the best chance to succeed. We have a whole chapter devoted to this in this book.

These variables and many others can increase or decrease the chances of divorce. They don't mean that you will, just that it makes it harder. The good news is that when you know these major variables, you can go into your second marriage with your eyes open, get the information you need to deal with these issues, and apply the advice you get.

As Denise and I go through this book, we are going to deal with the *real stuff*. It doesn't make sense to write a lofty book without real-world advice. We want to help you. We want to give you the tools to succeed.

Denise and I were both married before. I was married at 22 years old and married for twenty-seven years. My ex-wife and I have four wonderful children, one boy, and three girls, and now the grandchildren are starting to come. Denise was married for ten years, having gotten married at 31. She and her first husband have two beautiful girls.

After Denise got divorced, she sat down and wrote out a list of 23 traits she would want in her next husband. After we had been dating a while, she read them aloud to me. I met 22 of them. The good news was that the 23rd was something I could easily change, and I began what I called "Project 23." I wanted to be her "perfect man," or at least perfect for her, as there is no perfect spouse.

When I was looking for my future wife, I had six criteria that I was looking for in a woman, and Denise met all of them. She *was* the perfect wife for me!

What you are going to read in this book are the philosophies Denise and I believe in, the values that guide us, and the actions we take to make our marriage amazing. We are by no means perfect, but the fact that we are thinking these things through and applying strategies to succeed enables us to look forward to an amazing future!

There are many parts of this book that are specifically about a second marriage, but in many ways, it is simply a marriage book. The principles inside are ones that can make any marriage successful if applied. And, if you boil it down even further, this book is really a communication book, because communication is the number one skill and commitment spouses make to ensure that they have an amazing marriage!

How to Read This Book

Take some time to read through each chapter and reflect. Don't breeze through the whole book.

If you can, lie in bed together at night and take turns reading a chapter to each other. Then the next night, after thinking about the information from the night before, talk about what you thought or learned. Wait until the next night to proceed to the next chapter. Really talk about the issues. Get real. Share with your spouse what you really think. Be transparent. Be vulnerable.

So, let's dive in. Let's talk seriously and candidly about:

— Getting yourself healed from past relationships so you don't bring baggage to this one

— Picking the right mate

— Stepchildren and exes

— Money

— Communication and Listening

— Sex

— Meeting each other's needs

— How to handle conflict

And much more.

Don't Make the Same Mistake Twice

And by "mistake," I don't mean your spouse, I mean *you*! Let me explain ...

When you ask someone why they got divorced, you usually get something along the lines of, "He was a real jerk," or "She was crazy." And, because we know and like the person we are talking with, we simply take it at face value and assume they were married to an undesirable person who ruined their marriage.

Rarely will someone say, "Well, he did have his problems, but I wasn't a very good wife, and we decided to go our separate ways." It is human nature to blame others for our failures and mistakes.

The problem is that if that really is our position — that it was the other person's fault — then we are not living in full truth and we will miss an opportunity to grow and make the changes that will be required to make our second marriage amazing.

You remember the old saying, "It takes two to tango," right? Well, it takes two to ruin a marriage. Yes, one may be more at fault than the other, and very, very rarely one spouse may just go completely off the rails and ruin what was otherwise a great marriage, but in the vast majority of cases, *both people* played a significant role in the demise of the marriage.

So, it begs the question: What did you do in your last marriage that contributed to the downfall? In fact, relatively early on, I asked Denise, "What would your ex say was your fault in your marriage?"

She said, "Wow, great question." Then she did some reflection, and we talked about it. She asked me the same question and I gave her some answers. We both understood that when you step back and look at it objectively, we both played a role.

What this kind of question does is to *force self-awareness*. Self-awareness is the absolute key to knowing who you are and what you do that brings you successes and failures.

When you realize what negatives you contributed in your first marriage and you begin to grow and change, then — and only then — are you ready to move forward and give your best shot at an amazing second marriage. If you *don't* gain some self-awareness, then there is a very high chance that you will just drag those same bad habits, actions, thoughts, and philosophies into your second marriage. And your second spouse probably won't like them any more than your first spouse did.

Most people will think about what they want in a spouse. How many, though, will think about what their spouse may be looking for in them? Not many. Modern people do little self-reflection that brings about self-awareness, and yet self-awareness is the key to success in every area of life, including marriage.

After I got divorced, I took a lot of time for self-reflection. I was embarrassed and ashamed that I got divorced. It hurt like hell, just like it probably did for most of you. Even though I wanted out, it was still painful on many levels. I knew that I didn't want to be alone the rest of my life, so I knew that I had to come to grips with who I was and what I contributed that led to my divorce. It would be easy to pin all the blame on my ex-wife and point out the areas in which she failed, but that would only keep me mired in the muck and certainly wouldn't allow me to fix myself and grow to become a man who would be a better husband the next time around.

So what did I do? I read ... a lot. I went to counseling a few times a month. I met with friends of mine who are pastors. I have a close set of male friends who I stayed in touch with who helped me work things through. I decided that I was first going to need to understand myself; to know both my strengths and my weaknesses. Then I was going to work on my weaknesses so I could overcome them, and when the right time came, be an amazing husband for my future wife.

I found out a lot about myself. Here are just two of things I knew that I did wrong in my first marriage:

I didn't help out around the house much. My ex-wife did most of the household duties, and if something needed to be done that she couldn't do, I hired someone to do it. Now, we were in what most people would call a "traditional" marriage where the man ruled the roost, and my ex-wife was generally okay with that. In hindsight, I realize that I should have been much more engaged and involved around the home. I needed to change that for the future.

Secondly, I let my marriage become all about me. I was very well-known in our community; I became a world-renowned author and speaker. I made a lot of money. I had a big personality, and my ex-wife was the quiet type. Frankly, my ex-wife got lost in it all. And I wasn't perceptive enough to know that she had needs as well. Everything became about my needs. I needed to change that for the future.

I could give you many examples, but those are just two. There are many others. I knew that I needed to become a better man in order to become a better husband, and I would be looking for a woman who was transforming herself into becoming a better woman in order to become a better wife. I believe that our whole life should be about personal development and growth as a human being, but it is even more imperative when you are getting married for the second time, because if you haven't figured things out, grown and changed, then you are looking at becoming one of the 67% of second marriages that end in divorce.

How to Improve Your Self-Awareness

It takes some effort to come to self-awareness. The first thing is that you have to be willing to be honest. You have to be willing to look in the mirror, recognize the ugly truth and *change*. If you can't stand to know the ugly truth about yourself and admit your faults and weaknesses, then you aren't ready to change. You need counseling to get you to the point where it isn't overwhelming to know your weaknesses. Nobody takes joy in identifying their weaknesses. It's embarrassing and sometimes shameful. But we can take *hope* in knowing that when we do address our issues, we can change and live a richer, fuller life, including having an amazing second marriage!

So how do we do it? Here are some things you can do:

Read lots of books and listen to a lot of audio programs to improve yourself. Read books on personal development and self-growth. Listen to audios. Watch video lessons. Take a class. Get the information you need to expand your mind in these areas.

Go through my personal profile. Part of my business is personal coaching. I usually have seven to ten clients at a time, and the first thing I do with them is to send them a confidential personal profile that looks at their life from birth until now. It covers everything. Not only does this profile help them to reflect, it also helps me get to know where they have come from and what successes and failures they have had. I have included the questions from this profile at the end of the chapter.

Take a friend's evaluation. Evaluations are a tremendous resource to help us know where we have been and how to get where we want to be. One much-overlooked person who would give us a very insightful evaluation is our friend. Our friend? Yes! Think about it: They know you better than anyone other than your spouse. They see you in the greatest amount of diversity. They know about all the areas of your life. They could possibly give you the best evaluation you have ever had. So why do we need to do something formal like this? Why don't they just give us their thoughts throughout the relationship? Primarily because most friends won't, in the routine of our friendships, volunteer their true feelings, especially the ones they think we may perceive as negative. Most people simply keep their thoughts to themselves in order to keep the relationship "safe."

So there is a warning here. This is not for someone who would be offended by their friend's remarks. You need to go into this understanding that they care for you and have your best interests at heart and that you asked for the input! If you decide to go for it, there are some good questions to ask your friend(s). The full evaluation is at the end of this chapter.

Ultimately, coming to a greater sense of self-awareness is your choice. Making sure that you have done the work and come to grips with what didn't work for you in the past is key in making sure that your second marriage has the very best chance that it can be to become amazing. When you are partnered with a spouse who has and is doing the same, you become a powerful team and increase your chance for success!

Chris' Coaching Confidential Personal Profile (This is an excerpt containing the portions that will cause you to reflect)

— Years Married:

— Children:

— Is Father still living?

— Is Mother still living?

— If not, when did they pass away?

— How was your relationship with each of them?

— How did each of them influence you?

— Brothers and sisters. Please put in order of birth, including you.

— Briefly explain the family atmosphere growing up:

— What were any traumas you experienced while growing up?

— What were any memorable joys you experienced growing up?

— What is your religious background?

— Are you currently involved spiritually?

— How would you describe your general personality?

— What is your job history?

— Do you feel like you have gone up, down, or sideways?

— What are the most enjoyable things you have done professionally?

— What are your professional strengths?

— What are your professional weaknesses?

— Now the same two questions in regard to your personal life:

— How would you describe your health?

— Has this always been the case, or has it changed? When?

— What are your hobbies?

— How often do you pursue them?

— How would you describe your relationship with your spouse?

— With your children?

— How would you describe your financial status?

— Do you have any driving compulsions? i.e., to make money, etc.

— What are your primary fears at this stage in your life?

— Do you feel like you have lived up to others' expectations of your life? How?

— In the following categories, what would you like to achieve in the next year?

— Work:

— Family:

— Spiritual:

— Health:

— Financial:

— Relational:

— Intellectual:

— Emotional:

— What book(s) have impacted your life?

— What book(s) are you currently reading? What are you getting from them?

— What books are next on your "to read" list?

— Who do the people you currently surround yourself with inspire you to be?

— If you would change anything about your choice of people you choose to surround yourself with, what improvements would you make?

— What occupational goals do you have?

— Briefly, what is your occupational history?

— What are your greatest personal strengths?

— If you could improve one thing in your life that would dramatically improve all aspects, what would it be?

— What different leadership responsibilities do you have? (Career; Personal; Family; Community, etc.)

— What is your purpose in life?

— What is your mission in life?

— What does success look, feel, or sound like to you?

— What are you most grateful for? Why?

The Friend's Evaluation:

Give this to your friend, and when they are done, take them to lunch to go over it.

— What is my greatest strength as a person?

— What is my greatest strength as a professional?

— What are three issues you think I need to address in my life?

— What is my greatest weakness?

On a scale of 1-10, how do you feel I handle my money, given my desire for long-term financial health?

On a scale of 1-10, how do you feel I handle my health, given my desire for long-term physical health?

On a scale of 1-10, how do you feel I handle my emotions, given my desire for long-term financial health?

On a scale of 1-10, how do you feel I handle my spirituality, given my desire for long-term spiritual health?

On a scale of 1-10, how do you feel I handle my relationships, given my desire for long-term relational health?

In the preceding 5 questions, why did you answer as you did? What one thing do you think I could start doing today that would most drastically increase the quality of my life?

What one thing do you think I could stop doing today that would most drastically increase the quality of my life?

What is the biggest obstacle you think I will need to overcome in order to see my dreams come true?

You don't have to make the same mistake twice. You *can* change the course of your life and marriage. The second time *can* be better than the first. But it will require some self-awareness that you *choose* to gain for yourself. The more you and your spouse work toward understanding yourselves and the strengths and weaknesses you carry into the relationship, the easier it will be to create the amazing marriage we are all looking for!

Money, Sex and Power

These could be called the "big three" of problems faced in marriage. Each of these alone is a very powerful force in people's lives. Combine two or all three, and you have a powder keg waiting to explode if not handled properly.

Nearly 30 years ago, I read a book by that very same title, *Money, Sex, and Power*. I actually read it for the second time with a group of men in a book discussion group, and I still remember one man saying, "I wish I would have read this before I got married." Mind you, this was not a marriage book, but this man (and the rest of us after he said it) really had his eyes opened to the fact that money, sex and power are three of the biggest issues in a marriage — and three of the biggest reasons for divorce.

One of the things that I liked about the book is that it didn't come from the perspective that money, sex, and power are bad things. In fact, the author said they are both good and bad. Money, sex and power have what he called a "light side" and a "dark side." The point is easily made that money can be a good thing: You can provide for your family, take fun trips to see the world, and give generously to charities. But money can be a dark thing as well: You can be consumed by it, fearful of it, or use it to control people. Both sides of the coin can be seen with sex and power as well.

Money, sex, and power in marriage aren't any different. It can be a blessing, or it can be a curse. What are the deciding factors? Things like your individual perspectives on them, your communication about them, and how you come together to work as a team to give them the proper perspective in your relationship.

Given that these are the "big three," we wanted to take a look at each one individually.

Money

Issues over money have long been understood to be a primary factor in divorce, so if you want your second marriage to last, it is best to take the bull by the horns and address it both before and after you get married, and address it in a way that will produce positive results for your marriage.

Citibank released a survey that showed that 57% of respondents said that money problems were the primary reason for their divorce. 35% of a CNBC poll said that the primary stress in their marriage was money. Sonya Britt, a Kansas State University researcher, has concluded that arguing about money is the key indicator of who will get divorced.

OK, we agree on it: Money issues have the power to break a marriage. So how do we resolve money issues and how do we deal with them so that we feel like we are winning in our marriage?

Money seems so simple, and yet it is very complex. From the time we are little, we learn what to believe about money. Some of us are raised to believe that, "Money is the root of all evil." Others are raised to believe that it should be your goal in life to get rich. Just at a *belief* level, people come into marriages with very different perspectives that will be the cause of problems if not discussed and dealt with.

In many marriages, you have a spender and saver. One of you just lets the credit cards fly, and the other is constantly pinching pennies. You can see how that would cause problems. If this is you, guess what you have to do? Communicate and compromise. Focus on *solutions*.

What to talk about regarding money:

— What were you taught about money? Were you taught that money was good or bad?

— Your hopes and fears regarding money.

— Your financial goals. How much do you want to earn? How much do you want to save? How much do you want to have when you retire? Establish yearly goals for yourselves that you can go over year by year.

— What are your differences? Which one is the spender and which is the saver?

— Any changes that need to be made to accomplish your goals.

— Your budget. Agree together on what can be spent. Perhaps, if you have the resources, you give a certain amount that each person has access to as discretionary funds so the other doesn't have to worry about it.

— Compromise. There is a high likelihood that you will have to compromise on most of the above. Each of you thinks differently and has different needs and wants. Remember, though, that you are a team and both of you have to win in order for the team to win. One team member can't just bully the other into submission. Talk and compromise and negotiate until you come to a place of agreement.

Remember, *money* isn't the problem. It is how two people, given their differences but required to handle it together, handle money. Money is a tool, just like a hammer. It can be something that can build a house up or tear a house down. With one side of a hammer, you can pound nails that will construct a house that will last a lifetime. Turn that hammer around, and you can pull those nails out, leaving your home unstable.

Sex

In doing research for this book, I ran across an interesting article in the Huffington Post written by a divorced woman called "Eight Reasons Divorced Sex is Better

Than Married Sex." What I found most interesting about the article is that of the eight reasons she gave, only one of them, *No Strings Attached*, could be attributed to being divorced. The other seven, as you can see below, can all be true inside marriage! One could make the case that the "feeling like a teenager again" would be hard inside the marriage, but certainly not impossible, and, given my teenage experiences, I wondered why one would want to feel that way again. Here are the eight reasons she gave:

— Variety (different positions/places)

— Self-Esteem (how she felt about herself)

— No Strings Attached

— Fewer Inhibitions

— Feel Like a Teenager Again

— Fantasy Fulfillment

— No More Ruts (no more Monday, Wednesday, Friday scheduled sex)

— Sexual Knowledge (she knew more about sex at her age)

When we look through this list, we see that most of them could be *positive within a marriage*. In fact, one could easily assume that the real problem, if any or all of the above are issues, is that there is a combination of lack of communication, a breakdown in other parts of the relationship, and perhaps bad feelings toward your partner. These and other factors can play a role in causing the problems above. This then contributes to the breakdown in the marriage. These can all be fixed *inside* any marriage though!

When you are unwilling or unable to communicate your sexual desires to your partner, or they are unwilling to listen or care for those desires, it can hurt your sex life. When you are struggling in other areas of your relationship, it can make you desire sex less. When you have bad feelings toward your partner, such as resentment or anger, the last thing you want is to have sex with him or her.

All of these can be fixed by communication. In fact, great, meaningful sex, not just random sex for physical pleasure, is the culmination of communication and connection.

One of the premises of *Better the Second Time* is that both partners have to be committed to the growth of the marriage. They have to be fully engaged in the process and dedicated to the principle that they are in it together, to win.

Comparison and Projection

Two dangers that can affect people sexually in a second marriage are *comparison and projection*. Both of these are in relation to your past partner(s). When we get married again, we should do our best to start with a clean slate, but that can be difficult in all areas, especially sexually. This is mainly because sex is such a powerful force, and positive and negative sexual experiences can stay in the mind a long time. How we deal with these memories can either help or hinder your current marriage relationship.

Comparison. Someone who is getting married for the second time has had at least one other sexual partner, but in this day and age, it is common for people to have had many sexual partners, especially the older they are and the longer they have been single. According to the best research I could find, the average American will have sex with seven people in their lifetime. This brings challenges to a marriage if you are given to comparisons.

Comparisons are usually detrimental to a second marriage when you prefer a former partner sexually over your spouse. This not only *can* happen; it *does* happen. It doesn't mean that you want to be with that former partner, but it can still create problems in your marriage, especially if verbalized.

There are many things about your spouse that you may find yourself comparing to a former partner. It may be the way he or she made love to you, the lack of inhibitions, what they do or don't do, or even something like the size or shape of their genitals or breasts. It doesn't matter what it is. If you find yourself comparing your spouse to someone you have been with before, it is imperative that you deal with it, lest you risk the dangers that can come from letting those thoughts go too far.

Never verbalize your comparisons. This may seem obvious, but apparently it happens all too often. Saying things like, "I wish you touched me the way Mark used to," or "I really preferred larger breasts like Susan had," are going to be extremely damaging to your spouse and your marriage.

If you actually do have those preferences, there are two ways to take this on. First, and only if it is something that can be changed, tell your spouse. Do not, however, refer to a former lover. Show your spouse how you like to be touched, and when he does what you like, give him or her feedback that lets your spouse know they are pleasing you. Two, if it isn't something that they can change, focus instead on all of the positive reasons why you are with your spouse and not with that former lover who may have had what you liked in that one particular area.

Instead of focusing on the size of your wife's breasts, for example, remind yourself that you are with her because of the incredible woman she is, how she makes you feel outside the bedroom, the friendship and companionship that you share and other aspects of your relationship. That way, when you come together sexually, it becomes an intimate sexual expression of your outside-the-bedroom relationship. There is an extremely deep connection and bond that happens when this is the case. This is the difference between *making love* and *having sex.* Anyone can have sex. Two people deeply connected in their love for one another in all areas of their marriage *make love.*

Remember, this is a new relationship with a new spouse and will certainly be different because your spouse is a different person. Different can be better, so make sure that you are keeping an open mind to a new and more fulfilling sexual chemistry with your spouse. Perhaps you will find that the different sexual relationship you have is actually better!

Projections

Projections are the thoughts and mindsets we have that come from the negative sexual experiences we have had in the past. The more troubling or negative those experiences were, the harder they will be to let go.

For example, perhaps your first husband was a selfish lover and rarely, if ever, made sure that you were satisfied or had an orgasm during your love-making. Now, perhaps you are in a second marriage where you find yourself dissatisfied sexually. It would be easy to become disheartened and eventually bitter. You must first assume that your husband has good intentions. *Do not* project negative intentions on him. Instead, coach him. Talk to him. As we have already talked about, don't do it in a way that may make him defensive or feel inadequate, but in a way that allows him to hear you and to respond by trying to meet your needs. There is nothing more important to a man than having a happy wife. "Happy wife, happy life," is the common saying for a reason! A man wants to please his wife, both inside and outside the bedroom.

You and your spouse can have an amazing sex life — for the rest of your lives — if you commit to it. You must dedicate yourselves to maintaining the kind of overall relationship in which amazing sex thrives. This means growth in all areas so that when you and your spouse come together to make love, it is the celebration of what you have together as a whole. It is the sharing of the intimacy that you have both inside and outside the bedroom.

About Communication

So, let's talk about communication. In unhealthy relationships, one of two things usually happens. Either one or both partners don't share their thoughts and feelings, bottling them up until they explode, which leads to a negative experience, or, the partners don't feel like the other person listens to or validates their concerns. In positive relationships, both partners are dedicated to the communication process, even when it gets difficult and hard to get through. They know that *not talking* will be the death of them, while *openly and honestly communicating and listening* will help them build the kind of marriage they desire. It may be tough at times, but it is the only way to build a healthy marriage.

Now, how does this play out with sex? You have to talk about it. Let's take two examples from the benefits of sex the woman writing in *Huffington Post* said she could only get when she was single, and see how this could be easily fixed in a marriage.

Variety. We all know that life gets busy and we get distracted, and when the evening goes late, we just want to fall into bed, and thus, that is where most sex happens. It is even rooted in our language: *We went to bed together.* But the bed isn't the only place to have sex. It will take some creativity and some forethought, but this is easy to fix. Get creative!

Perhaps you are craving some variety. Tell your spouse. Now, don't say, "How come we only have sex in bed? You aren't very creative." This would cause defensiveness. Instead, *invite* them to join you. Something like "You know, it would be super sexy to make love on the couch tonight," is much more inviting. Or, if your spouse is lying on the couch one evening, make your move. You are accomplishing a few things here. One, you are communicating that you want some variety. Two, you are communicating that you want to make love to your partner. Three, you are suggesting an agenda for having sex on the couch (or wherever else you may want, for that matter).

Fewer Inhibitions/Fantasy Fulfillment. I actually found this one interesting because the natural way of thinking about this would be that it would be much easier to share your inhibitions and fulfill your fantasies within the context of a safe and loving relationship than with someone you barely know and who you don't know you can trust. If you are cultivating a loving, open and trusting relationship as a whole in your marriage, overcoming your inhibitions and sharing your fantasies will come much easier, making your marriage *amazing*!

As we have said repeatedly, people are different. We know that. Spouses are different. They have different tastes and likes in food, clothing, and yes, even sex. So the key is ... communication! Are you getting it yet?

Some people like sex in the morning, some at night. Some like the lights on, others off. Some like to be on top, others on the bottom. Some like oral sex and others don't. Some people want to be tied up, and others can't even imagine that! There is no right or wrong; there is only personal preference. The key is to talk about it. Open up to your partner and tell him or her what you would like. If your spouse doesn't know, then he or she can't respond in kind and come together with you to improve your sex life.

Many people are scared or ashamed at what they might like to try and will hold back, even from their spouse. Successful couples talk, listen, understand and apply what they communicate about.

It is good to sit down and talk about your sex life with your partner from time to time, preferably somewhere far from the bedroom. Have a conversation when you aren't in the throes of passion. Here are some things to talk about with your partner:

— Talk about how you are feeling about your sex life.

— Talk about what you would like your sex life to become.

— Talk about how often you would like to have sex.

— Talk about what you love that your spouse does to/with you when making love.

— Talk about the things that you don't like that your partner does.

— Talk about any fantasies that you may have or variations you would like to try.

There are two keys that will make this work. First, the speaker: You have to be willing to speak your mind, being honest, forthright, authentic and transparent, speaking in a way that won't lend itself to causing your partner to become defensive. Two, the listener: You must be willing to listen, hear (there is a difference), internalize, not interrupt, and then respond lovingly.

Remember, you are a team. When you are talking together, you are working on your team winning the game. You aren't trying to point out how your partner failed or why you are so unfulfilled. You are focusing on exciting successes that you two can experience together.

Sex is *powerful*. We know that. It can be a force for greatness in your marriage. It is a bond that you only have with your spouse. While making love, you give them a part of you that no one else gets. They see you in your most vulnerable state: naked. In a healthy relationship, that creates a bond that makes your marriage even more amazing!

Power

When we use the word power, we may regard it as synonymous with control. So for the sake of our discussion in this area, we will call it power or control.

When we are babies, we have no power. In fact, if someone weren't caring for us, we would die. When we are growing up, we do not have much power or control. Our parents make most of the decisions for us. As we get older, our parents release control over us, allowing us to become increasingly autonomous and making more and more of the decisions for ourselves. Then comes that day we all remember. We are finally, totally autonomous! We eat what we want, we go where we want, and we go to bed and get up when we want. We finally have total control of our lives, and we answer to no one!

Then we get married. Marriage is a combination of independence and *interdependence.* Technically, yes, we can still do "whatever we want," but now we have pledged to build a life together with another person, who most likely has very different ideas about how things should be done, at least in a few areas. This is a struggle for most people.

Say a single man makes $50,000 a year. That's *his* money. He earned it, and he can do what he wants with it. Now when said single man gets married, it is no longer *his* money, but *their* money. The money that comes into the house is the couple's money. He can no longer just do what he wants with it because he has an obligation that he willingly entered into with another person. Now he must work with his spouse to decide what will be done with the money. And that's just an example of money. Things like work, and whether one spouse will stay home and raise the kids, how to raise the children, what religion, if any, the children should be raised, where to live, how much of a mortgage to take out ... the points of potential conflict and the struggle for power are nearly endless in a marriage.

The first thing that must be addressed is your philosophy on power, control, and decision-making in the marriage. Most modern marriages get started with well-meaning people who say that they are a "50-50 partnership." There is no leader. But what happens when they both feel strongly and they disagree? What if the wife gets an incredible job offer in her field, but it means they would have to uproot and move across the country? She definitely wants to because it has been her dream and he absolutely does *not* want to because he likes his house, his city, and his job right where he is, thank you very much. What happens then?

My position is that there has to be a leader. I have written many books on leadership, and have studied it extensively for 30 years. As one of my friends so succinctly put it once, "When have you ever seen co-CEO's work out?"

There must be a power structure, or at least definition of roles in a successful marriage. Don't worry; I'm not saying that you have to have a traditionally "patriarchal" based marriage, though that works for some and if the wife is happy with letting her husband have the final say on issues, then good for them. I am instead suggesting that you and your spouse communicate clearly and often about who will hold what power and what will happen when a stalemate arises. Whatever you two work out in that regard is great if it works for your marriage.

The most powerful way to break the stranglehold of power struggles is through the concept of *servanthood*. Remember, you are a team, and both of you have to win in order for the marriage to win. If one person wields power over the other, the one who lacks the power can begin to feel used, uncared for, and ultimately, resentful. The one with power may get his or her way, but they may end up in divorce court.

Servanthood is about serving your spouse or considering your spouse's interests as more important than your own. Sacrificing for your spouse. Letting them have their way. Now, this works powerfully when *both* spouses are doing it. The fear is that if we are serving, our spouse will become a taker. That is a danger, of course, but not if both spouses are approaching the relationship trying their best to serve the other and meet his or her needs. Now, there isn't a struggle for power. There is the power of service. When both spouses commit to this concept and seek to live it, it goes a long way toward keeping power struggles at bay.

As with both money and sex, the key to keeping power and control issues from harming your marriage is communication. Proactively discuss these issues and share any concerns with your spouse.

Here are some things to discuss regarding power and control:

— How will decisions get made in your marriage? What will be the process in place for making big decisions?

— Who will have the final say in a decision that has to be made? If you are uncomfortable giving that to one person, how will the decision get made?

— Who will make the day-to-day decisions about finances?

— Who will make the day-to-day decisions about the children?

— In the bigger picture, beyond the day-to-day, who will make the decisions on these issues?

Final Thoughts on Money, Sex, and Power

As you can surmise after reading this chapter, the primary way to make sure that money, sex, and power don't become issues for you is to communicate effectively, clearly, and often! Communicate until you get on the same page and come to an agreement, or at least a compromise that both people feel comfortable with.

Keeping money, sex, and power from becoming issues requires self-awareness. It is good for us to not only communicate with our spouses about these topics but to also do some deep reflection on our own perspectives. Getting clear with any bad philosophies we may have regarding these and how they may be affecting our marriage is the very first order.

When two people get on the same page, money will never be an issue, no matter what your income. There are people who are rich who still fight about money, and there are poor people who don't fight about money. When two people get on the same page about their sex life, sex becomes an incredibly powerful force for intimacy and pleasure in the marriage, keeping them connected on a deeper level. When two people get on the same page with power, control and how decisions will be made in a marriage, they rid themselves of the infighting that comes when two people who are supposed to be on the same side aren't, and they become a tightly cohesive couple who can take on the world!

There is an old proverb that I love: *One can put a thousand to flight, but two can put ten thousand to flight.* One person can be effective, but two people, aligned in their lives, can be effective exponentially!

Love Languages and Meeting Your Spouse's Deepest Needs

We wanted to include some thoughts in this chapter on the most significant points made in three of my favorite marriage books I have ever read. They are *The Five Love Languages* by Gary Chapman, *His Needs, Her Needs*, by Willard Harley Jr, and *Love and Respect* by Emmerson Eggerichs.

The Five Love Languages is a book that teaches you the five basic "languages" that you can learn to "speak" to your spouse to meet his or her needs.

His Needs, Her Needs is a list of the five strongest emotional needs of both men and women in relationships.

Love and Respect is based on the theory that a woman most wants love from her husband and a man most wants respect from his wife.

As I go through my thoughts on each of these books, I think it will give us plenty to think about as it relates to how we can help meet the deepest needs of our spouse. Now, one might think, *it isn't my job to meet my spouse's needs. He/She should be fulfilled in and of him/herself.* This is faulty thinking and the kind that may leave your spouse feeling empty and contribute to the breakdown of your marriage.

The marriage relationship is obviously a unique relationship. It is the closest of all human relationships. There is something mystical and spiritual about it. It is a *union*. Historical Christian teaching has used the term describing how a couple "becomes one flesh."

When we commit to another person, we are called upon to take seriously how we may meet one another's needs. No person is an island unto himself. We all have needs, and many of those needs cannot be met by ourselves. In marriage, we have that special relationship with another person who can bring fulfillment to those needs, like two pieces of the puzzle coming together to complete the whole picture.

As you go through these lists, take time to read and contemplate them. Talk to your spouse about them. In the case of *The Five Love Languages*, figure out which one or two are your spouse's and learn to communicate to them using their love language.

Since an amazing marriage is predicated on ever-growing people, learning and applying what they learn, I would encourage you to get one or all of these books and go through them with your spouse.

With that, let's take a look at the principles of each of these three books.

The Five Love Languages

Chapman's book says that there are certain things that *speak* to our spouse. These are the love languages that make our spouse feel loved and cared for. The languages that Chapman writes about are:

— Gift-Giving

— Quality Time

— Words of Affirmation

— Acts of Service

— Physical Touch

As you read through these, can you see how one or two of those might be more important to you than the others? The same is true for your spouse. The importance of this is that when we speak our spouse's love language is when they feel best. Of course, different people have different languages. One issue that arises is that often one spouse will speak the language they like best, but it isn't the language that their spouse enjoys the most. You may love words of affirmation, and so you speak words of affirmation to your spouse when in fact they would feel much more love, care and attention if you would clean out the dishwasher (an act of service).

One of the most powerful dynamics of my and Denise's relationship is that we share the same top two love languages. That makes it easy for us to speak the other's language. Both Denise and I have Words of Affirmation and Physical Touch (which includes but is not limited to sexual touch) as our top two. So if you could hear our conversations and read our texts to each other, you would see a lot of affirmation of one another. She and I are regularly articulating something positive we feel about the other person, and that keeps us emotionally filled and satisfied. We both gain energy from physical touch. Holding hands, a soft touch of the other's back, a quick neck rub and the like are simple ways throughout the day to speak the other's love language and meet their needs.

Chapman talks about keeping your spouse's *emotional tank* full. When we speak our spouse's love language, they feel loved and come to a more fulfilling emotional state about themselves, you, and your marriage.

Let's take a look at each one and see what they mean.

Gift-Giving. Some people just love to get gifts. When you give a gift to them, they get excited. They love the whole process, the surprise, the unwrapping, everything. These don't have to be big gifts either. They can be small gifts. Whether it is a small, inexpensive item you know they will love and use or something expensive that's a real luxury, it doesn't matter. A gift says that you were thinking of them, you know what they like and you took the time to go and get it for them and deliver it to them.

Quality Time. There is time, and there is *quality time*. Just because you spent the afternoon alone together in the house doesn't mean that you had quality time. Quality time is time spent together with your spouse in a way that he or she considers it high value. It means giving your spouse your undivided attention. It means talking, listening and effectively communicating. It could also mean that if your spouse loves riding bikes that you take a few hours and go riding with them. Whether you talk or not during the trip, your spouse will consider it quality time that you went with them. Now for my soapbox: Meals should be quality time. Put down your phone; enjoy your food and the company of your spouse! Unless you are rushing to get to the kids' game and your dinner consists of fast food eaten while driving, meals are supposed to be quality time and represent an everyday opportunity to have some.

Words of Affirmation. There is an old proverb that says that the "tongue has the power of life and death." Our words are *powerful*. So true, especially for those who have words of affirmation as their love language. These words can be expressed in various ways, but they should be expressed regularly. Denise loves a small Post-It note on the mirror that says, "I love you," or "You are beautiful." Those are words of affirmation. When Denise and I were living halfway across the country from each other when we first started dating, I would try to text her during the day what I loved about her or admired her for. That is the key: Try to think about what you love about your spouse and communicate those to your spouse. Guys, "You are beautiful" is great and no woman will ever turn down hearing it, but we need to work harder and expand our words of praise. Things that cover the gamut like "I really appreciate what a hard worker you are," "You are such an amazing and patient mother," and "You did such an incredible job organizing that school fundraiser. I'm so proud of you," will go a long way. Ladies, telling your man "I appreciate how you provide for our family," "I think you are so funny (or intelligent or whatever)," and "I love how you make me feel when you are making love to me. You're an incredible lover," will make your husband feel like he can take on the world!

Acts of Service. Serving others means that you are thinking of ways to help them. How can you serve and help your spouse? Obviously doing chores is an easy answer. Unload the dishwasher, take out the garbage, clean the barbecue or shovel the driveway. But what else? Maybe get up early and make your spouse's lunch and pack it for him or her. If your spouse normally pays the bills at the end of the month but dreads it, grab them a couple of days early and do your thing with the checkbook. Tell your spouse to sleep in and you will take the kids to school today. Guys, cook your wife a meal. And I don't mean a romantic meal which will send the message that you are looking for a little action later on. Just get home early and cook a meal so that when she and the kids get home, she doesn't have that burden on her. When she walks in, hand her a glass of wine, have the TV turned on to HGTV and tell her dinner will be ready in 20 minutes.

Physical Touch. It probably doesn't need to be said since we're all adults here, but physical touch is not exclusively sexual touch. In fact, non-sexual touch will go a long way toward making sure that when you are engaged in sexual touch, the fires are burning bright. When you wake up in the morning, reach over and rub your spouse's back before getting out of bed to jump in the shower. Sneak up behind your wife in the kitchen and give her a hug from behind. Give your wife a foot rub while you are watching TV. Run your hands through your husband's hair while he's on a phone call. Hold hands while you are walking through the mall. Put your arm around your spouse at the football game. Any time you can share a short, meaningful moment of physical touch, it will make your spouse feel loved.

The keys here are:

Know your spouse's love language

Make the effort to speak your spouse's love language on a daily basis.

Oh, and before we close, just let me say that I have a sixth love language. Oatmeal cookies. Just make me some oatmeal cookies, and I will feel loved!

His Needs, Her Needs

His Needs, Her Needs is one of the first marriage/relationship books I ever read, and it is a good one. It was published quite some time ago, and it can feel a little dated, but the principal lessons are very good. First, you have to start with the premise that men and women are different, so if you don't believe that, you may have a problem with it, but I'll guess that most of us are on the same page with that concept.

Harley describes the five general and basic needs of each of the sexes as this:

Her Needs:

— Affection

— Intimate Conversation

— Honesty and Openness

— Financial Support

— Family Commitment

His Needs:

— Sexual Fulfillment

— Recreational Companionship

— Physical Attractiveness

— Domestic Support

— Admiration

Let's take a deeper look at each.

Hers:

Affection. Men, your wife needs affection. Affection doesn't mean sex, although that is part of it. She needs your soft touch. She needs you to hug her and hold her. Reach out and hold her hand while you're driving. Touch her softly. Tickle her a little bit (if she doesn't mind being tickled). Run your fingers through her hair while you're watching TV together. Speak lovingly. Listen intently. Tell her you love her.

Intimate Conversation. "How was your day?" isn't intimate conversation. You have small talk and chit chat, and then you have deep, meaningful conversation that connects a husband and wife at a deeper level. Women love to talk about how they feel and what they think. They love to talk about your relationship. Engage her in this and make that deep connection, meeting her need. Men tend to like to keep conversations short and at a 30,000-foot level. Your wife will love it if you will set aside some time to have deeper, more meaningful conversation where your attention is focused on her.

Honesty and Openness. We men, as a general stereotype, are not big talkers. We aren't very open. We don't like transparency because it makes us feel vulnerable. But our wives value those things. And frankly, we men need to learn to become more open and honest. One note about honesty. It doesn't mean that we aren't honest, but more that we aren't candidly honest. Not that we lie to our wives, but that we *omit* information and don't like to talk about it. Your wife is wired differently, and by engaging her in these kinds of interactions, you will connect with her in a deeper way because you will be meeting her needs.

Financial Support. This is one of those that some may say is culturally irrelevant from when this book was originally written, but it still holds true in the vast majority of homes. Many women today are very self-sufficient and don't need a man's money. For example, Denise has a very high-paying career and made more than enough money to provide for her home and children before I met her. She was completely self-sufficient. A woman does, however, want a man to be there for the family financially. If the wife stays home with the kids, she feels secure if her husband is providing well for the needs of the family. When he isn't, she feels a lack of security and feels in need. Unfortunately, there are too many men who don't work hard, make poor financial decisions and take away that feeling of financial support from their wives.

Family Commitment. Many men view themselves as a provider and that is important, but all too often, when a woman says she doesn't feel loved, a husband will say, "What do you mean? I go off every day, working sixty hours a week so I can provide this home, take you on vacation and pay for the kids to go to soccer camp." That's not what she's saying. What she is saying is she wants you to be her husband, not just her provider. She wants you to be the children's dad, not just the one who pays for their school clothes. She wants you to be there and to be *present* mentally and emotionally when you are there.

His:

Sexual Fulfillment. Of course, this is a broad, sweeping generality, but statistically, it is relevant that men want sex more often than their wives. This isn't a right or a wrong but simply a fact of biology for most couples. I've worked closely with thousands of men over the years, and the number one complaint about wives is that they don't want to have sex as much as the husband. Ladies, I'd like you to think about something. When your husband committed to you, he committed to having sex with only you. When you realize that he is off the market, it means that this need can only be met by you. One of the top ways you can meet his needs is to make sure that he is fulfilled in this area.

Recreational Companionship. Most men I have worked with would *love* to have a spouse who enjoyed doing things together with them. Common interests are powerful in a relationship. Yes, men want alone time with their male friends, but they also have a strong desire to have time just "kicking around" or doing an activity together. Working to find some activity that you both enjoy so you can be his recreational companion will be much appreciated by your husband.

Physical Attractiveness. Let's start with a given that your husband already thinks you are attractive or he most likely wouldn't have pursued you in the first place. This isn't about being a bombshell. It is about doing the most with what you have. It means keeping yourself up. It means being fit and living a healthy lifestyle. It means that you don't spend all day, every day in sweatpants and a T-shirt. Men love pretty things, so make yourself pretty. Do your nails and hair. Smell good. Again, this doesn't have to be a huge production. Taking a little time each day to put some finishing touches on will be very attractive to your husband.

Domestic Support. This may be the one that causes the most controversy or feels the most out of date in a day and age where many homes are dual-income homes. The man and woman both go off to work, and it isn't like the wife is staying at home all day and has the time and responsibility to do all the domestic chores. That being said, it is important to have discussions and come to agreements on responsibilities. One thing to note on this, ladies, is that your husband probably wasn't taught all of the skill sets needed to do some of the things needed around the house. Traditionally, these things were passed on from mother to daughter, and many sons weren't even taught how to do them. Ironing comes to mind. So one thing you can do if splitting chores is to show him how to do it and encourage him when he does it right.

Admiration. Women, if you only knew how much your husband thrives on your admiration! Actually, he lives for it. Your husband, even if he would never articulate it this way, wants to be that knight in shining armor for you. He wants to be a man who you look at and are impressed by. One of the most powerful things you can do for your husband is to express your admiration for him. Take him in your arms, look him right in the eye and tell him what you admire about him. And if you want to put the admiration factor on steroids, tell other people what you admire about him! When the two of you are out with a group of people, sing his praises to the group. His spirit will soar, I promise you!

Love and Respect

Love and Respect is a very simple concept. Even so, it is perhaps the best marriage book, or book on male-female relationships, I've read in a very long time; specifically because it nails the two primary needs a man and a woman in relationships have. The author is a Christian counselor, and one day passed over a Bible verse that he had read many times over. This time something jumped out to him. The passage said that husbands should love their wives, and wives should respect their husbands. The author wondered for the first time why it didn't just say that husbands and wives should love each other — why the different instruction for each spouse?

After doing extensive research, he found out that women value being and feeling loved the most, while men value being respected the most. What he found out was that men need to love their wives and show it, and women need to respect their husbands and show it!

He describes a cycle. The cycle can either be good, or it can be "energizing." A good cycle has the husband loving his wife. In return, she feels loved and shows her husband the respect he desires. Feeling respected, he shows her his love even more ... and the cycle continues.

Then there is the *crazy cycle*. The husband doesn't feel respected, so he withdraws and doesn't demonstrate his love for his wife. Feeling unloved, she shows him disrespect ... and the cycle continues.

The author says the key is to recognize when you are on the crazy cycle and to get off that cycle and onto the energizing cycle by making purposeful and unconditional demonstrations of love and respect. Someone has to break the cycle.

So, if a wife treats her husband with disrespect, he is going to feel hurt and will be tempted to withdraw. That will only perpetuate the crazy cycle, so he must instead show her unconditional love and love her in spite of how he feels. That will fill her need for love and will move her toward showing him respect, putting them on the good cycle instead of the crazy cycle. And of course, the reverse could be demonstrated with the roles reversed. When feeling unloved, the wife would seek to show unconditional respect and bring her husband to the place of showing love again and getting them on the energizing cycle.

You can see from the overview of these three books that the key element is to look at your spouse and see what really makes him or her tick. Whether it is one of his or her *love languages*, his or her *needs*, or simply the love or respect that he or she desires, we as their spouse can meet those needs purposefully, helping our spouse to be fulfilled and giving us the enjoyment of being in a more loving and happy marriage.

As we close this chapter, I would encourage you to buy these three books and go through them with your spouse. At the very least, buy one of them that seems most interesting and dig through it, then focus on your part of the equation.

Listening: The Forgotten Key to Effective Communication

The word "communicating" implies talking. For example, if I said, "I was communicating with Joe the other day," you might assume that I was talking with him or maybe emailing him. Either way, you would assume that I was sending information Joe's way. Of course, this is completely legitimate, but at the same time entirely inadequate. Communication is not just what we say. In fact, I would say that a far more important skill to master if you want an amazing marriage is how to listen rather than how to talk. Listening is the forgotten key to true communication.

The natural tendency is to talk, especially if you are feeling angry or defensive. We want to lash out and make sure that our spouse knows how we feel. What would happen in a marriage if we could fight and overcome our natural urge to speak and instead make a purposeful commitment to listen to our partner? I believe it would be revolutionary. Imagine what would happen the next time you were angry at your partner because of something he or she did, and instead of lashing out, you asked if you could have a few moments and said to them, "I'm trying to understand something. Yesterday you (fill in the blank), and I'm wondering why you did that. Can you help me understand what your line of thinking was?" The conversation would take on a completely different tone than if you just launched into an attack because you've already decided your spouse needs to hear how you feel.

Assume good intentions on your partner's communication. One of the things that causes problems is that when our spouse begins to speak to us, particularly during conflict, we assume they are "out to get us," even if unknowingly or subconsciously. So we become defensive, and we are now in what we would consider attacker/defender positions. And then we just play the roles until someone is hurt. But there is a better way. Simply assume that your spouse wants what is best for you and that he or she wants to make this conversation a win-win, even though they may have to talk about something tough. Denise and I take this principle very seriously, and on more than one occasion it has helped us to thwart or cut short what could have been a much bigger and tougher conversation. Change your mindset and beliefs to believe that your spouse is communicating with good intentions for both of you.

Just don't talk. This may sound simple, but just keep quiet. So often we aren't really listening, but rather we are waiting for our spouse to take a breath so we can jump in and counter their assertions. Instead, tell yourself that when your spouse begins to speak, you are not going to say a word until he or she is completely done speaking and they have given you at least three seconds of silence. Forcing yourself to be quiet is an excellent tool for communication, because now you have essentially committed to doing nothing else but listening.

Give your full attention. Don't be looking around. Don't be thinking of something else. Don't be on your phone. Don't be trying to figure out what you are going to say next to prove your spouse wrong. Look them in the eyes and really focus and listen. If you're in the middle of something when your spouse wants to talk, and you feel it would be too tough to focus, ask them if can wait until another arranged time when you know you will be able to give your full attention to the conversation. Whatever you do, be present, engaged and fully devoted to the conversation.

Express positive body language. When someone is talking to you, they are usually looking at you, and what they see can have a significant effect on how the conversation goes. What does your spouse see when they are trying to communicate with you? Do they see someone with his or her arms crossed and their body turned away from them? Do they see someone with their head in their hands? Or do they see someone seated directly across from them, face turned toward them, body and hands in an open position, looking them directly in the eyes? Each of these body language positions will communicate something back to your spouse and will affect him or her in a positive or negative way and will have a significant impact on the overall tone and outcome of the conversation.

Take it at face value. Just take your spouse for what he or she says. Don't make assumptions or extrapolations. For example, if your husband says, "I'm not a big fan of this dinner," he means he doesn't like that specific meal. That's it at face value. But what we do quite often is respond with something like this, "I thought you liked my cooking. When did you stop liking how I cook? You used to like my meals." We place other meaning on communication that is never intended by the person speaking the words. Don't read into things. If you suspect something, then you can ask, but don't come to any conclusions until you hear your spouse say those words. Taking conversation at face value goes a long way toward keeping conversation clear, concise and understandable.

Ask questions. If you do suspect that perhaps your spouse is trying to say or insinuate something rather than what they are saying, simply ask rather than assume. To use the illustration above, when your spouse says, "I'm not a big fan of this meal," and you think there may be a value statement underneath, just respond with something like, "I hear you saying you don't like this meal. Are you saying you dislike all of my meals?" At this point, your spouse will most likely say, "No, honey! I love your cooking! It's just something about this one meal." See what happened there? They spoke at face value; you didn't know if you could take it at face value, so you asked a clarifying question that allowed your spouse the opportunity to confirm that indeed, nothing to fear, they meant nothing more than they didn't particularly like this one meal.

Empathize. Empathy is putting yourself in the place of your spouse. Perhaps your spouse is, for whatever reason, fearful of or uncomfortable telling you what they are about to tell you. Being in tune with that will help you be a better listener as you show the proper response to whatever mood or place your spouse is coming from.

Sometimes if we would empathize we would find ourselves in a much more compassionate place with our spouse rather than a defensive or judgmental place, and that is going to make the conversations you have around your home go much better.

Don't retaliate. Whatever you do, *do not retaliate.* Conversations don't usually start out in a yelling match. Instead, they take steps to get there, and each spouse contributes to the steps. Here is the good news: You have full control. At any point, you can decide not to provide the next step in the escalation process. Let's say that your spouse is angry with you and she hits you with an unfair or inaccurate accusation. You have a choice. One, you can ignore it and let it go, maybe even saying something like, "I don't think that is a fair assessment of me, but I hear your overall point." Or you can ignore it and then if you feel it needs to be discussed, you can bring it up at a later point with something like, "The other day you said such and such. Did you really think that or were you just speaking out of anger?" Either of these will deal with the issue but not make it worse. What you absolutely do not want to do is retaliate with something like, "How in the world can you say that I do that? You do *far* worse than that when you do such and such." That is just an escalation and an open invitation for your spouse to take the conversation to an even angrier level.

Reflect back to confirm the communication. When your spouse has finished speaking, both throughout the conversation and at the end, it is always good to reflect back what you think you heard them say. I know that "What I hear you saying is ..." or "Let me clarify. Are you saying ..." can sound trite, but statements like these work. It allows you to say what you think he or she said and gives them an opportunity to clarify or confirm, putting you both on the same page, which is exactly where you want to be in a healthy relationship.

Communication is tough, even among people who love each other and who want to communicate well. It takes practice, but implementing the above principles and tactics will go a long way toward helping you, and your spouse become much better listeners and communicators.

How to Fight *Right*

Every couple "fights." Now, fighting looks different from couple to couple, but conflict is bound to come, no matter what. You can take two of the nicest people on earth, who truly love each other, and if you lock them in a 2,000-square-foot box for any period of time, there will be conflict. I actually had a guy tell me that in 20 years of marriage, he and his wife had never had a fight. My first thought was that either he was lying or that he or his wife wasn't being forthright in their feelings or opinions. *Everybody* fights.

Fighting is something we must embrace as an aspect of marriage that must be navigated since it has the capacity to destroy a marriage over time if not handled appropriately and constructively. Done right, dealing with conflict can actually bring about a stronger marriage through working together, seeking common ground and extending forgiveness. Done wrong, and for an extended period of time, fighting can destroy a person's self-esteem, willingness to be transparent and vulnerable, and ultimately the marriage itself.

The first thing I want to reiterate is that there is *never* a win-lose situation in a marriage. There is only win-win and lose-lose in a marriage. If one partner "wins" and the other "loses," the partner who "won," didn't really win. A marriage is a team and a partnership, not a one-on-one competition. For example, in boxing, you have a fight. The goal of each fighter is to win by points or by knockout. When the bell rings, each boxer seeks to harm the other. When the fight is over, the winner gets the money, the belt and the accolades.

Not true with marriage. If one "wins," they may be left with the smug sense that they won, but they are left with a spouse who lost, and that has ramifications for the overall relationship. It doesn't make it better; it makes it worse.

In a fight, you may have someone who is right, but through the fight, it is important that both sides are heard and understood so the relationship is held in high esteem and regard. The *totality* of the relationship is far more important than the single fight, disagreement or conflict you are currently in. As the old saying goes,

"You can win the battle, but lose the war." That is a quote every married person should memorize and remind him or herself of when entering into conflict with his or her spouse.

I'll give you a recent example that Denise and I experienced. I had assumed some things and spoke to Denise about them. First off, I assumed wrongly, and that was the first step of conflict. As we talked, it was a little tense, but not too bad. I quickly realized that I had made some wrong assumptions and that my concern was unwarranted, so I quickly asked for forgiveness. It seemed to be over, but something kept stewing in me. I wasn't still upset about what had happened, but rather how I felt during the interaction. I hadn't felt heard about the general sense of what I was concerned about, so I brought it up with Denise again. To her credit, she knows that if one person in the relationship has concerns, it is important to discuss them and to get through them. She listened intently, and as I explained it to her, she saw how I might have felt unheard. She apologized for that, and everything was dealt with. I recognized that I had misjudged something, and she recognized that in the discussion, it was more important to come together than to simply make me know I was wrong.

That is a basic example of how two people can have a disagreement that could lead to conflict or a fight, but we both went into the exchange with some underlying principles and goals:

— We love the other person.

— We trust the other person.

— We want to understand the other person.

— We want what is best for the other person.

— We assume the other person has good intentions for our relationship and will act accordingly.

— We will speak directly, transparently, authentically and humbly.

— We will speak and act in a way that honors, loves and respects the other person.

— We will seek solutions in a positive atmosphere.

— We will seek to conclude the fight in a way that both people feel as though they won.

Now, believe me, these are strong and beautiful ideals, but difficult to abide by when we get into conflict because a human being's nature is to fight to win! A self-aware couple will do their best to keep these principles in mind and practice as they navigate their fighting and conflict.

So, how do we "fight right," so to speak? Here are some tips for keeping conflict to a minimum and for keeping the conflict you have positive.

— **Handling Anger** - Anger is normal. It isn't wrong to be angry. Anger is a legitimate human emotion, and we should understand and accept that sometimes our spouse will be angry about something. The absolute key thought here is that anger must be appropriate. Anger can let our spouse know that this is a *big deal*! And if it is a big deal to my spouse, it should be a big deal to me as well, at least in how I interact with her about it. Anger, while a legitimate emotion, should never get out of control. That means yelling, cursing, putting your spouse down, throwing things, and of course, physical violence. If things are getting heated and anger is becoming inappropriate, it is best to take a "Time-Out," which I explain below. If an anger problem is recurring, then counseling is the best option.

— **Choose to Speak Positively** - How you speak is a choice. It doesn't matter if you are angry or upset, you can still control it. Here is a perfect example: You and your spouse are in a heated argument, with voices raised. The doorbell rings. You open the door, and in your best sing-songy voice say, "Sue, so great to see you!" Even though you are angry, you still chose to speak to Sue at your door in a positive way. You have total control over how you speak. Now, what would happen if we utilized that same control to speak to our spouse the same way, no matter how we feel? It would be powerful!

— **Seeking Understanding** - It is natural for almost everybody to want to make sure they are understood. It is a defense mechanism. When someone confronts us, we rarely start by asking them to explain more so we can gain better insight. In fact, most of us just jump right into explaining why they are wrong and why we are right. Stephen Covey, the author of *The Seven Habits of Highly Effective People*, gave us this principle: *Seek First to Understand, Then to be Understood*. Could you imagine how much marital conflict would be avoided or kept to acceptable levels if couples simply implemented this one principle? You wouldn't talk or defend or seek to explain yourself until you first completely understood your partner's position.

— **Embracing Compromise** - Notice I didn't say "*accept* compromise." Accepting compromise could come across as though you don't really like it, but you have to do what you have to do. Compromise, however, is a *great* thing. It keeps both people happy and working together, knowing that while they may not always get their way, they usually get most of what they want and their spouse is working with them to come to positive solutions and outcomes. This is why smart couples *embrace* compromise because it is a means to a very positive end: An Amazing Marriage!

— **Establish the "Time-Out" Option** - Let's face it, sometimes it is just best to stop. One or both of you is getting riled up and emotions are beginning to break, and the conversation is likely to go south quickly. It is at this point that one of you simply says, "I'd like a time-out." This must be immediately accepted by the other spouse with the understanding that this isn't the end of the discussion, but just a pause that allows both of you to cool down. One important aspect of this is that before the time-out takes place, you agree on when you will pick the conversation back up. Perhaps it is in twenty minutes, or perhaps it is after the children go to bed later in the evening. This allows you to know that there will be some finality to the issue.

— **Talk About One Issue at a Time** - I call them rabbit trails. You know, you're talking about a specific issue and one of you feels trapped, so you bring up another issue completely. I get it. It is a defense mechanism. When this happens, it is simple to say, "OK, I would be happy to talk with you about that if it is an issue. Let's finish this topic and then we can bring that up." Sometimes people fall into a *tit-for-tat* discussion. You bring up something your spouse did, and they come back with, "Well, you did this or that last week." Again, not beneficial to the current discussion. Something similar to the strategy above would be good, "OK, let's talk about that next. I want to make sure you get heard on that, but can we discuss this first?"

— **Don't Cross the Line** - This is *anything* that would harm your spouse. Being unfair, cursing, name-calling, attacking their character, etc. It seems like this shouldn't even have to be a discussion because, after all, these are two people who are deeply in love with one another and have pledged their lives together, but it happens all the time. The problem is that once you cross the line, it is hard to walk it back. You can't unsay things. And once you cross the line, it is easier to cross the line the next time and even push the line further.

— **Allow Each Person the Time to Speak Uninterrupted** - You know the drill. You are waiting for your spouse to take a breath so you can jump in and say your piece. Then you can't wait any longer, so you interrupt. Then your spouse interrupts, and the next thing you know you're talking over one another and interrupting each other. No one is listening, so nothing is being accomplished. Try the technique of simply letting the other person talk until he or she is completely finished. Then repeat back to them what you think you heard them say. If you didn't get it, let them talk again. If you got it, then it is your turn to respond. This requires that both people be committed to the process and the technique. Done properly, this can be very powerful, keeping your fights unemotional, and can even shorten the time spent in the conflict.

— **Keep Body Language Open and Loving** - It is hard to be mad at someone who is tenderly holding your hand, isn't it? Body language and what we do with our posture during a conflict can add to it or defuse it. When we cross our arms and turn our backs, we are essentially saying to the other person that we don't care what they have to say. And how can a relationship get better when one person doesn't care what the other has to say? What does it say, however, when we are turned fully toward our spouse, looking him or her in the eye and intently listening? It says that "even though there may be an issue, I am with you. We are a team, and I care about how you feel." Be purposeful about how you hold yourself and your body language when you are interacting with your spouse during a conflict. Let your body demonstrate that you are open, present, and listening, seeking a positive resolution.

— **Establish a "Key Takeaway" from the Interaction** - When the conflict is over, it is important to get the key takeaway. Maybe it is that you shouldn't have made assumptions, or that there needs to be more discussion when making a decision about the kids. Talk about it. Ask your spouse what he or she thinks is the key takeaway. Come to some agreements on what you can learn from the interaction.

— **Establish Action Points to Change What Caused the Fight** - This is the "to do" list, or perhaps the "not to do" list. Once you have the key takeaways, you can look at the actual behaviors that caused the tension in the first place. If it was something you did, make sure you set your intention to not do it again. If it was something you didn't do, set your intention to do what is right in the future.

Fighting in a marriage is okay, and to be expected. The difference between people who have normal marriages and those who have *amazing* marriages is that people with amazing marriages learn how to fight right. Take some time to go through this chapter with your spouse and come to some agreements on the ground rules and strategies you will use in your next fight so that you come out of it with a win-win situation that makes your marriage stronger.

Forgiveness

One of the most powerful things you and your spouse must master in order to create and maintain a healthy marriage is *forgiveness.*

The word *forgive* is defined in Merriam-Webster as "to cease to feel resentment against an offender," and "to give up resent of or claim to requital."

The fact is, your spouse will absolutely, unequivocally offend harm or wrong you. There is one hundred percent chance of this. And, of course, you will do the same to your spouse. It happens because we are humans, and humans are selfish and imperfect. It happens even with the ones we love the most. We love them with all of our heart, and yet, from time to time, we make a mistake, blow up, or do something that hurts our partner.

What happens next will determine to a great degree how your marriage goes.

To not forgive will lead you along a path of resentment and bitterness. You will start counting offenses and bringing them up in the oncoming warfare you will experience. Your marriage will dissolve into bickering, infighting, and tit for tat arguments. Your memory bank will store every wrong your spouse commits and use them in the future to win your fights. Or ...

You can *forgive*.

If you forgive you will sow seeds of peace, love and understanding. You will throw your spouse's past behavior overboard and not count it against him or her. That will lead your relationship to be one of love, joy and happiness.

So, what is forgiveness based on? I really believe that forgiveness is based on deep self-awareness. Self-awareness? Yes. Here is why. When we know ourselves, we know that we too are imperfect and harm others. Because of that, we want forgiveness when we do it. We tend to treat others differently. When someone wrongs us, we want *justice, compensation, and retribution.* However, when we wrong someone else, what do we hope for? *Grace, mercy and forgiveness.*

So, if we become self-aware, we see that in order to have integrity, we must act toward others the way we want them to act toward us. This is the meaning of the Golden Rule: Do to others what you would want them to do to you. So, if we want forgiveness, we must *give* forgiveness.

Second, we must understand that marriages that practice forgiveness survive, and those that don't will fail. Your choice. Do you want to hold onto things and have your marriage die, or do you want to truly let things go and have a flourishing marriage for a lifetime?

Third, you must understand what a lack of forgiveness does *to you*. Studies are conclusive that those who don't forgive others harm their own mental and emotional state. They become bitter and resentful. To paraphrase the old saying, *to not forgive someone else is like drinking poison and expecting the other person to die.*

So, how does forgiving actually work? What is the practical outplaying of this? Here are some thoughts.

First, your spouse must be on board and be in agreement. Sit down and talk to your spouse and verbally commit to making forgiveness a foundation of your marriage.

Second, there are two parts to the most whole way of forgiving. It requires two people. The first is the offender. He or she should ask for forgiveness when the wrong is realized. It goes something like this: "I'm really sorry that I became angry with you and snapped at you. You don't deserve to be treated that way, and I want to do better. Will you forgive me?" Do you see what happened there? There was recognition of the wrong, a statement of what they hope to strive for, and a direct ask for forgiveness."

Then you have the response. A simple, "Of course I forgive you," is perfect.

That being said, sometimes forgiveness is a one-way street. Sometimes the other person won't recognize that they did something, or they won't agree with you when confronted with it. What then? You can still forgive. Forgiveness works best when both parties are working together, but forgiveness can be given solely by the person who was offended. It is still *your choice.*

Forgiveness is a decision. Sure, it can sometimes be a hard decision given the gravity of the offense, but it is still a decision nonetheless. We must *choose* to give up holding something against the person who has harmed us. We must release what they have done and the anger, bitterness, etc. that it causes in us.

Then there is another trick to help you forgive. You see, there is *passive* forgiveness, where you would just make the decision in your head, and then there is what I call *active* forgiveness. It stems from a Bible passage that says, "If your enemy is hungry, feed him, and if he is thirsty, give him something to drink. In doing this, you will be heaping burning coals on his head." Now, your spouse isn't the enemy, and you don't want to heap burning coals on his head, but I think you get the point.

I'll tell you a story about how one woman I knew used this principle. She lived in an apartment, and the people above her were always noisy and banging on the floor. She would use the broom and pound on the ceiling to no avail and even talked to them about how noisy they were, again, with no results. Then she decided to love them. She was a great cook and specialized in desserts. Every time she baked cookies, she baked an extra helping for her upstairs neighbors. Every time she baked a pie or a cake, she made one extra to take upstairs. Guess what happened? Yep, her neighbors quieted down!

So, maybe your spouse is really getting at you. Our typical response may be to respond in kind, but instead, we should respond with even greater kindness and shock them into seeing how they have treated us. Try it and see if it doesn't elicit more kindness and better behavior out of your spouse!

Remember these things as you think about forgiveness:

- — Forgiveness is needed by everyone.

- — Forgiveness is a choice.

- — Talk with your spouse about implementing forgiveness into your relationship.

- — Forgiveness is a foundation of a healthy marriage.

- — There is both *passive* and *active* forgiveness.

Don't Let an Ex Steal Your *Amazing* Marriage

Ah, the ex. Exes have a bad reputation, but they aren't all bad people, and they don't all cause problems. Exes are like everybody else in that there is a wide variety of them. Some will be fine to deal with, and others will be terrible to deal with. Most will be somewhere in between those two extremes. Another variable in regard to how much you will have to deal with your spouse's ex is if they have children together and how old the children are.

The key is to keep a strong marriage relationship between you and your spouse; one that cannot be disrupted by a former spouse. Another key is to understand who you are dealing with and developing the best philosophies and strategies for dealing with your spouse's ex that will be the best for maintaining the best relationship possible.

The fact is, the only reason you know this person is because of a negative situation that happened between your spouse and this person in the past. That means that chances are very slim that you are ever going to have a great relationship with your spouse's ex, because the whole situation was born out of negative circumstances. There is a great Bible passage that says, "As much as it is up to you, live at peace with everyone." That is good advice for us. We control ourselves and not the other person. We can control ourselves but only set boundaries for the other.

I decided when I came into Denise and her girls' lives that I was going to take a proactive approach and positive attitude toward Denise's ex. They had been together sixteen years and married ten of those years, and had been divorced five years when I met Denise. The girls were fifteen and seventeen, which meant that there was only going to be about three years before the girls would both be in college and it would basically just be Denise and me in the home. In the meantime, since the girls were still in the home, it meant that Denise and her ex were co-parenting and doing their best to raise the girls.

I, of course, didn't know Denise's ex and had only heard the stories from the past. However, I told Denise that I was going to start with her ex at ground zero, our relationship being based solely on what was between him and me, and nothing else. I wanted to start out with a specific worldview in regard to her ex:

We would start at ground zero.

I would treat him with respect.

I would honor his role as the girl's father and never encroach on that.

There wouldn't be a problem unless he created one.

Let's face it; this whole situation in a second marriage is awkward at best. There are so many moving parts, and most of those parts are rusty and broken. This is about a group of people trying to deal with a situation that isn't the situation anybody thought they would find themselves in.

Here are some things you should keep in mind when dealing with your spouse's ex and seeking to establish a good working relationship with him or her.

Don't compare yourself. This can be a temptation for many, but it really shouldn't be. We can find ourselves wondering if we are as good as our spouse's ex in a variety of areas — do we make as much money, are we as good looking, are we as good in bed, whatever — but this is nothing but a very bad idea. The fact is that there are probably at least a few areas in which your spouse's ex *is* better than you. We all have our strengths, and we all have our weaknesses. But here is the key point: Your spouse is **with you!** Even if your spouse's ex made more money than you, for example, it wasn't enough to keep your spouse happy and to keep their marriage from falling apart. So the comparison is a moot point. All comparing yourself does is give you the opportunity to get into a funk.

Set clear boundaries. Exes need boundaries. Your spouse has moved on and chosen to live his or her life with you. Now their ex is someone they have to deal with, to some degree, but those dealings are within boundaries. There is an excellent book called *Boundaries*, and I love the analogy that people are like properties. Your neighbor owns his property and can do with it what he wants. If he wants a big ugly structure on his property, it is his, and he can do it. You may think it's ugly, but it's on his property. But what if he decides to construct something on *your* property? This would never happen, as it would mean that he had encroached on your property boundaries. The same is true of your spouse's ex. They can be crazy all they want, just not when they are with you. There are boundaries.

Let's look at some examples — abusive behavior, for starters. Perhaps an ex treats your spouse with verbal abuse, either in person or on the phone or via email or text. This is unacceptable, and boundaries must be set. They need to be told that it will not be tolerated. If they don't abide by those boundaries, then there have to be consequences that you determine. Another example would be not to let them invade your home time. If an ex is texting your spouse at five in the morning or ten at night, your spouse doesn't have to respond. The ex can be told that they can text and expect a response during reasonable hours of the day. You shouldn't have to worry about your spouse's ex interrupting your family dinner time. Basically, what you wouldn't tolerate from anyone else, you don't tolerate from your spouse's ex.

Set a united front with your current spouse. As I have reiterated over and over again, you and your spouse are a team. It is you two against the world! There is no one closer to you than your spouse. Anyone or anything that tries to get in between you two or cause problems is the enemy. That may seem like strong language to you, but your marriage is sacred and to be protected at all costs. You and your spouse must let your spouse's ex know that you two are sealed together as a team, and that means nothing will come between you.

Don't get in the middle. To a certain degree, your spouse and his or her ex need to go on with their interactions without your interference. If it doesn't affect you, stay out of it. If they want to negotiate where the children are going and when, let them do it. It only concerns you if it affects you. If your spouse needs your strength, encouragement or advice, then he or she can ask you, and you can jump in. Otherwise, let them deal with it.

Treat them with respect. I believe that all humans should be given the courtesy of respect. Even if your spouse has told you horror stories about their marriage, your spouse's ex is still a valuable human who that is worthy of respect. This is exactly how I started out in my intention with Denise's ex. He is a former civil servant, a successful businessman, and the father of two girls I have come to love as my own. Me treating him with respect is good for everyone and allowed us to start at ground zero. They are going to be much more likely to respond positively if you show them respect than if you treat them with disdain.

Empathize with them. No matter what the circumstances and no matter who was more at fault in the demise of your spouse's former marriage, your spouse and his or her ex went through the wringer when they got divorced, just as most people who get divorced do. Your spouse's ex may still be dealing with and struggling with that fact. Now, to be sure, this is a very enlightened mentality and approach to take, but again, we are talking about how to have an amazing second marriage, not a mediocre one, and that means dealing with exes in the most positive way possible. Having some sense of empathy for your spouse's ex will go a long way in being patient and tolerant as you work to make all of the details work out.

Your attitude is your choice. Ultimately, your attitude is your choice. Your attitude toward your spouse's ex and the situation you are in is your choice. You chose to marry someone who was married before. You went into it knowing what you were up against, and everything that may come into play. Now you can choose to have a positive attitude and make the most of it. Will it be perfect? Nope, but life never is. That doesn't mean you can't have a positive attitude about the situation. My experience is that your attitude has a significant effect on the outcomes you experience.

If possible, develop a personal relationship with the ex. This may be asking a lot, but if at all possible, develop your own relationship with your spouse's ex. I had an uncle, my mom's brother, who got divorced from my aunt and married another woman. My aunt and my uncle's second wife developed a working relationship that eventually turned into a friendship. I distinctly remember a family reunion I held at my home long after my uncle had died, and my aunt and my uncle's second wife drove to the reunion together! Now, this certainly doesn't mean that you have to hang out together, but having a positive relationship with your spouse's ex will go a long way toward having an amazing marriage because you will eliminate a lot of the negatives that go with a bad relationship with the ex.

Find positive aspects about your spouse's ex and praise them for those qualities. I believe that anybody can find something positive about someone else. If your husband's ex-wife is a good mom, tell her that! If she decorates her home well, tell her that! If the brownies she made for the kids for after the last football game were incredibly delicious, tell her that. People feed off of the praise of others, and your spouse's ex is no different. Find something positive and focus on that, and you may see some of the negatives slip away.

These are just some basic tips for developing a good, working relationship with your spouse's ex. Remember, we are all just trying to get through life, we all hit bumps in the road, and we all just want to find happiness and joy along the way. Regardless of what has happened in the past, let your life be a beacon of light and hope along the way. This includes how you interact with your spouse's ex.

How to Be An Amazing Stepparent

After I had raised four children of my own, I met Denise and her two incredible daughters. Suddenly, I wasn't done. Now I was a stepfather with teens in the house! I had to make sure that I gave some serious thought to how to be an amazing stepfather to these two beautiful young women, since I would now have a role within their lives.

This is where it gets tricky, and frankly, I had it easy. The two girls are excellent students, involved in Varsity dance, and very responsible and respectful. Their dad is a good guy and is cordial with Denise, and he and I get along quite well. It is about as good as you could hope for. I know that for others, it can be a lot more complicated depending on the circumstances.

Being a stepparent and how that plays out is heavily dependent on the circumstances. Think about how each of these would be different.

— Your spouse has one child who is twenty-four years old and married.

— Your spouse is a widow/widower with three children under the age of five.

— Your spouse has two children, ages eight and 10, who are both developmentally challenged.

— Your spouse has an angry ex who constantly tries to use the children as a political football.

— Your spouse has rebellious teens who are involved with drugs.

You get the point. Each of these would have their own challenges and opportunities. For example, to compare the first two of the situations, in the first, you would never try to exert any sort of authority in the life of your stepchild. You would take the role of a friend, and perhaps even a mentor. In the second situation, however, you most certainly would take on the full role of the traditional parent. The children would spend most of their childhood looking at you as their parent and authority figure.

For me, I knew my role was simple. I had only a few things I set out to do:

— Love their mom and show them how a man should treat a woman.

— Encourage and support them in their endeavors.

— Offer advice *if and when asked.*

— Support their mom in her decisions as the authority figure in their lives.

— Encourage the girls to have the best relationship possible with their dad.

That's really it. I didn't have a tough job or situation like so many of you do. I understand that it can be difficult, but let me encourage you: *It is worth it, and you can have an amazing marriage no matter what your situation!*

With that said, let me give you some general thoughts on how to be an amazing stepparent.

Be great to your spouse. First and foremost, your primary relationship is with your spouse. The children will eventually move out of the house and it will be just the two of you. The best thing you can do is love your spouse, treat him or her exceedingly well, and be an example of a great marriage for the children. An amazing marriage will provide the peace and stability that is imperative for children.

Limit your expectations. I would say that you should go into the relationship with your stepchildren with very few expectations. Don't focus on what they should do or how the relationship should be. Rather, focus on your core values and actions and take care of what you know you should do.

Remember, you are not a replacement parent. You are not their mother or father. You are secondary in that role to their birth father or mother. There are a few exceptions to this, such as if the parent has passed away or is totally absent, or perhaps in some cases imprisoned. You should always honor, to the best of your ability, the relationship between the children and their biological parent. Find good things about their parent and speak about those with the children.

Decide what your role will be. Again, this will depend a great deal on the situation, ages of the children, the availability of the father or mother, etc. No matter what the situation, make sure you sit down with your spouse and spend time talking about what your role should be. Frankly, your spouse should be the one who leads in what the role should be, and you should serve your spouse by fulfilling that role.

Understand and support your spouse and his or her ex's parenting plan. Most exes have some sort of parenting plan or agreement that is at least loosely held to. The kids are theirs, and the responsibility for their wellbeing is theirs — your job is to let that happen. Of course, you should be able to express your thoughts if you think that something could be better, but these should only be suggested, and the decision whether to implement is for your spouse and their ex to decide.

Get to know your stepchildren. To the degree that you can, get to know your stepchildren. Take them out to dinner. Go to their events. Ask lots of questions. Listen! Listening and putting it in your memory bank will go a long way toward building a relationship. Show that you care about what they care about. Don't be critical, just accept. For example, if they like a certain kind of music, don't say, "Why do you like that crap?" even if it *is* crap! Know them, accept them, and love them!

Empower your stepchild(ren) to set the pace for how fast the relationship will develop. Don't try to force a relationship. You have the rest of your lives to create a strong, healthy and loving relationship with your spouse's children, so just let it happen. Chances are, they may be skeptical or even a little fearful, and it may take some time. When we got married, I tried to put myself into Denise's girls' shoes. One day it is just them and their mom and then, **BAM!** Now there is a guy in the house! Of course, they knew me, and we had a great relationship, but it is still something that everybody had to get used to. In our case, there was one more person who had to be considered. That is a big adjustment for anyone, let alone children. Relax and take it slow and easy.

Be their cheerleader. Your stepchildren have gone through a divorce, too. Without getting into a debate about the long-term effects on children of divorce, suffice it to say that they didn't ask for the situation they are in, and they most assuredly could use an extra helping of encouragement. They have already gone through enough discouragement and disappointment. You can be their cheerleader. Focus on the positive, and be supportive!

Don't be a welcome mat. With all the talk of supporting your spouse and letting them be the leader and being your stepchildren's cheerleader, you could get the idea that I am suggesting that you be a doormat. Not at all! You are an adult, and you deserve respect and honor as an adult in the home. This is best earned rather than demanded, but if, for example, you have wild and disrespectful teenagers in the home, you and your spouse need to come up with a plan and strategy to make sure that the children are expected to act appropriately.

Have regular family meetings. I suppose this is especially true the younger the children are, but even with kids in their late teens, this is a good idea. It doesn't have to be a formal meeting if you have dinner together frequently enough to have the proper time to talk family issues over. If you have a very busy family, it may require scheduled time. This time should be used to go over schedules, talk freely and openly about any concerns that you, your spouse or the children may have and anything else that is pertinent to the health and wellbeing of the family.

Allow plenty of "alone time" with your spouse and his or her children. Remember, your stepchildren used to have the full attention of their mom or dad. Now they don't. Now their mom or dad is investing a considerable amount of time and energy into you. That can be hard on a child. Understand that fact and encourage your spouse to spend alone time with his or her children. Yes, of course, there will be lots of family events where you all are present, but your stepchildren will greatly appreciate you being supportive of them spending quality time with their mom or dad. You can even facilitate it by buying tickets to an event that your spouse and his or her children would enjoy going to together. Your stepchildren will see that and love that you are fostering that relationship with their mom or dad!

One could go on forever with tips, tricks and strategies for being a better stepparent, but these are a great place to start, and for the most part would put you a long way ahead of where most stepparents are in their relationship with their stepchildren.

Take some time and go through this with your spouse and have good, candid discussions about how you can be the best stepparent possible!

Fueling the Fire

What is it that we always hear?

Relationships start out hot, and then once you get married and reality sets in, everything becomes normal.

I want to completely challenge this theory that almost everyone buys into. What is "reality?" What is "normal?" Why does something have to start out exciting and then become boring and mundane? I would suggest that it doesn't. Could you imagine if we used this logic in any other area of our lives?

Well, I started out really physically fit but then reality set in and I just got fatter and fatter. That's just the way it goes, and there is nothing I can do about it.

We started out with a million dollars in the bank, but then the everyday routine hit, and we went broke. That's just the way it goes, and there is nothing we can do about it.

You get the point.

The everyday reality that we experience in all areas of our lives is based on the choices we make. Just as your physical fitness and your financial state are governed by the choices you make, it is the same with our marriages. Every day that a couple wakes up, the state of their marriage is exactly what they decide it will be. Any day can be good or bad. There is no universal rule that says because you've been married for years, your marriage has to be boring or unfulfilling.

I think one of the best analogies for the trajectory of a relationship — and how to keep the trajectory going up — is a simple fire.

A relationship usually starts like a campfire filled with very flammable dry sticks. Touch a match to it, and it lights right up, burning fast and hot. The twigs get the logs started, and soon enough, you have a blazing fire. Everything seems easy, and everybody is happy.

But what happens if you just let that raging fire burn with no attention to it? It slows down to a moderate fire, then to small flames, then to burning embers and then the fire goes out. This is, I believe, the natural course in so many relationships. They miss out on the fundamental principle that would keep their marriage burning brightly: Give your marriage attention. And even more specifically:

Do something daily. With a fire, if you want it to burn brightly and keep you warm, you have to regularly add more wood to the fire and use the poker to move the logs into positions that will facilitate a better burn. Think about it, though. How many other areas of our lives do we have to work daily — or at least regularly — to keep going in a positive upward trajectory? Staying physically fit requires regular and strenuous workouts. Achieving financial independence requires spending discipline and regular investments. Keeping your yard looking good requires tending to the grass and the garden.

Why then wouldn't we understand that a marriage is something that we have to work on regularly and more importantly, daily? Why wouldn't we understand that it doesn't have to be some major attempt every day, but that even small daily efforts will keep your marriage strong and burning brightly?

So this begs the question: Are you *willing* to work each and every day to make your marriage a priority so that you can keep the flames burning bright? Unfortunately, for many, the answer is no. They simply won't make the effort. For a smaller group of people, like those of you reading this book, they will experience an amazing marriage because they will not suffer from the steady decline of their marriage.

One of my favorite quotes of all time is from Jim Rohn: "Everyone must experience one of two pains, the pain of discipline or the pain of regret." This is so true. To commit ourselves each and every day to invest in our spouse and marriage can feel like discipline. It may not always be easy. We may have to go out of our way or make time that we don't feel like we have to give. But we do it anyway. And if we do allow ourselves to experience the "pain of discipline," we will not have to experience the pain of regret. Those who will not discipline themselves each day will one day experience the pain of regret. They will get to a place where their marriage is almost out and ask themselves, *Why didn't I tend to the fires of my marriage? Why didn't I work to keep the fire burning brightly?*

In the rest of the chapter, I would like to give you some thoughts and ideas on ways that you can keep your marriage fire burning brightly. I've divided them into two categories, non-sexual ways to keep the fire burning brightly, and ways to keep your sex life on fire.

Non-Sexual

Know your spouse. One of the things that will keep a deep connection is to know your spouse better. It is always surprising to me to see how many spouses — even those who have been married for a long time — don't know basic information about their spouse, like what their favorite color is, let alone what their biggest dreams or darkest fears are. When you know someone deeply, you have a deeper connection, and the fire burns brighter. Be sure to go through the appendix on 45 Questions to Help You Get to Know Your Spouse Better.

Hold hands more often. There is something very tender about holding hands. It provides connection. It provides safety. It says "I love you," and "I want to be close to you." To paraphrase the old telephone company commercial, "Reach out and touch your spouse!"

Focus on what you love about your spouse. It is very easy to focus on what you don't like about your spouse. When they do something that annoys us, it triggers us to think about that. That is all "focus" is — thinking about something. You have thoughts going through your head all day, and when you are thinking of something, you are focusing on it. What you focus on has an effect on how you feel. If you focus on your spouse's negative traits, you will feel negative about them. If you focus on your spouse's positive traits, you will feel positive, and the fire will burn brighter.

Eliminate those things that put the fire out. First, figure out what the wet blankets are that put out the fire in your marriage. There are some obvious ones, such as the little annoying things we do that drive our spouse bonkers. I'm always amazed when a person knows what he or she does that their spouse hates and yet they keep on doing it. When Denise tells me that something annoys her, I make it my goal to stop. Why keep on doing things that will just pick at the happiness of your spouse and the happiness of the marriage? On an even deeper level, things like putting your partner down and speaking negatively should be abandoned at all costs.

Carve out time to spend with your partner. Time is like the size of the fireplace in our analogy. You need to spend time with your spouse so as to interact and get those fires burning. Unfortunately, we live in the busiest time of human history. Think about it for a moment. Just

150 years ago, what did a couple's day look like? They got up on the farm, ate breakfast together, the wife tended to the home while the husband went to the field to work, he came back for lunch then continued in the afternoon, then they ate dinner together and had nothing else left to do but be together during the evening. The next day they repeated that, and so on for 50 years. Not so today. We are extraordinarily busy and have hundreds of options about how we can spend our time each day. This is why it is *absolutely imperative* that we are *purposeful* in setting aside time to spend with our spouse. This keeps us from drifting apart.

Date nights. One of the simplest ways to set aside time is to have a weekly, or regular, date night with your spouse. Why does dating have to end when the rings get slipped on? This is especially true of couples with children. It is too easy to get so into parenting that you forget to invest in your marriage. What I'm about to say may be a bit controversial for some of you, but hear me out: Your spouse and you are the core of your family. Your children are add-ons. Eventually, your children are going to grow up and leave your family unit and start their own with someone else, leaving — you guessed it — just you and your spouse. But so many couples lose themselves in their kids and don't keep the fires going that when the kids leave, they don't know the other person, feel any passion, and for millions of couples, this ends in divorce. Make your spouse your primary focus and make sure you are dating them and spending time with them! There are tons of books and online resources to help you keep your dating life fresh with ideas. Use them!

Flirt more. It probably has to be said, if only for the guys reading this, that flirting can be flirting just for flirting's sake and doesn't have to lead to sex. It can be, however, in and of itself, very hot and keep those fires burning. In a sense, this is fun teasing. It could mean a text from a husband to his wife while he's in a business meeting that says, "I'm thinking about how sexy you are." It could be a wife walking past her husband while he is on the couch and looking seductively at him when she catches his gaze. You get it. You know how to do it. Flirt more!

Give up selfishness. Selfishness is the silent killer. Ultimately, when we act selfishly, we kill off the fires of our marriage. Our spouse won't like it and will feel used or resentful. When we act *selflessly*, however, that is hot for our spouse, and the fire burns brighter. In all areas of our relationship, we should always be thinking about how we can consider our spouse's interests more important than our own. Imagine what would happen if both spouses acted this way toward each other all the time? Powerful! The fires would burn *hot*!

Sexual

Massages. Who doesn't like a massage? You don't have to be a licensed massage practitioner to make your spouse say, "ahhhh." This can be as simple as a five- or ten-minute shoulder massage as he or she sits in front of you while you watch TV to a full body massage with a good lotion. Maybe this will lead to great sex, maybe not. Either way is good and will stoke the sensual fires.

Practice being more emotionally vulnerable during sex. I hate to break it to you, but sex is not just physical, despite what current culture may tell you. Maybe for animals, it is, but the human being is a multi-dimensional being, and sex is far beyond the physical. Sex is emotional. Sex is psychological. Sexual is spiritual. This is why, I believe, we have so many problems around sexuality today — our society views it as something that is simply physical. "Oh, it was just sex ..." they say. Unfortunately, there is no such thing as "just sex." But there is a great upside to the depth of sex. Sex is a *great* way to deepen your connection. Yes, there are a lot of times when you want to just rip your clothes off and go at it, but there is a place — an important place — for emotional sex. A time when you move slowly, and you look deeply into your spouse's eyes and speak tender, emotional words. I know this is difficult for many of you who don't even communicate that way with your clothes on, let alone with your clothes off, but this is something to work on.

Sexy texts. While you are both gone during the day, there is no reason you can't throw a few twigs or branches on the fire so when you get home together, the fire is burning bright. Tell your spouse something sexy about him or her. Tell them a naughty thought you were having about him or her. Remind him or her about a very sexy time you two had that you were reminiscing about. Go ahead, let your imagination run wild. One very interesting idea I ran across was to have the two of you write a story together, one sentence at a time and then turn it over to your spouse to continue and so on. You may start with, "I had just put the kids to bed," and your husband responds with, "and you heard the bathwater running ..." Her: "As I walked into the bathroom, it smelled incredible..." Him: "I had scented candles going and rose petals on the floor...." Then take it from there. You and your spouse can create any situation that makes you happy — and you should!

Allow tension to build. You know how some nights it is early on and things are already heating up? Maybe it's only 6 o'clock, but the kids are gone for the evening staying overnight at friends' houses. Take your time. Don't just jump right into it even though it is heating up. Take a break. Cook dinner together, teasing each other as you do. Make it romantic, drag it out a little and let the tension build for an amazing connection later on.

Candles and mood. This takes effort, but that's what this whole chapter is about: effort. One candle is not a mood enhancer. Twenty candles is a mood enhancer. Maybe some incense. Certainly some music. Make a playlist of your sexiest songs. Most hotels now have music channels on the TVs that you can turn to a certain genre if you search a little bit. Maybe some colored lights would do the trick. Whatever it may be, make an effort to set the mood. Your spouse will feel very special when he or she walks into that room, and you surprise him or her with the effort you put into making your night spectacular.

Maintain a sense of curiosity about sexual intimacy. Sex should be explored between you and your spouse. Sex doesn't have to be missionary style every time. Change the flavor. It is up to the two of you, and frankly, it is my belief that if the two of you enjoy it and both consent, have at it. It may not be my cup of tea, but it doesn't have to be. Be curious. Expand your mind. Try new things. If you like them, add them to your repertoire. If you don't, no need to do it again.

Vary the kind of sex you have. The same things every time become boring and predictable. Three kisses, he touches her there, she grabs him there, off comes the last of the clothes, etc. Don't get me wrong, the physical sensation and the ultimate orgasms that happen feel great, but remember, sex is also mental so varying things up will keep the mind engaged. You *want* your spouse to think, *Whoa! Where did that come from? I like THAT!* Missionary sex in the bed every single time becomes predictable. Change the place, change the pace, change the positions... just change it up.

Make sex a priority. Think of it this way: Sex is *glue*. Sex, along with other aspects you are working on, will hold your marriage together. We are sexual beings, and given the right atmosphere, sex can — and should — be hot! "But our schedules... I'm tired... my job... the kids..." I know, I know. But you and your spouse's marriage is a priority if you want it to last and be amazing, so you have to make it a priority. You know, when I was at my fittest — much thinner and more muscular, my workouts were actually in my calendar. Every day they were blocked out in time. They were a priority, and I benefited from the prioritization. The same is true of sex with our spouse. We *must* make sure that it happens, and happens regularly. It will take some work, especially for you young couples who have little children. Both Denise and I have been through that stage of life and know what you are going through. But with discipline and effort, you can make sure that it happens, and I am telling you, you will be glad that you made the effort.

Change your pattern of who initiates sex. Typically in a relationship, one person is most often the initiator and the other the responder. This is good if the initiator is sensitive to timing, and if the responder is open to rewarding the initiator's efforts. But it is also good if the responder regularly changes things up and initiates. I don't think it has to be 50-50 per se, but even if it is twenty percent of the time, it will change things up and will also encourage the regular initiator.

Kiss longer. Yep, kiss longer. Remember when you were a teenager and sex wasn't an option (or at least as much as it is when you're married)? You would have MARATHON make-out sessions, kissing for hours. Now when you're married? For many, it is two on the mouth, two on the neck and away you go... What would happen if you just focused on kissing a little (or a lot) longer?

Remember how you felt as a teen? Maybe you'll get that feeling back!

More time with foreplay. The most uncomfortable presentation I ever had to sit through was when my mother invited me out to her 35-foot sailboat she lived on in the marina at Bainbridge Island, Washington. I was months away from getting married, and my mom had a very specific talk she wanted to have with me. Without going into all the details — even though in hindsight they were very funny — my mother wanted to make sure that I "took care of" my wife-to-be sexually. And the key to that was *foreplay*. I essentially got the anti-Wham-Bam-Thank-You-Ma'am talk that night. And you know what? I'm glad I got that talk. Specifically for us men, we need to work on warming our wife up and giving her time. But more foreplay is good for both spouses to work on, and it will certainly enhance the sexual experience for both of you.

These are just some of the many thoughts that can help you keep the fires burning bright in your marriage. The key, as we have mentioned before, is that it takes work to keep the fire fueled and the flames burning brightly!

Appendix A - How to Pick the Perfect Spouse for You

There is no such thing as a perfect spouse, but there can be a perfect spouse *for you.* One of the things that both Denise and I did before we met each other was to create a list of the things we were looking for in our future partner. Denise made her list six years before she met me, and I made my list two years before I met her. Now, if you are already married, these may be a moot point because we would certainly never encourage you to go looking again, but rather to utilize the tips and strategies you found in this book to make your marriage with your spouse into an *amazing* marriage. If, however, you found this book and you are still single, these lists may give you some food for thought.

Denise's list of attributes she was looking for in her future spouse:

— He is faithful to me.

— He believes in God and practices his faith.

— He has initiative/motivation.

— He has a higher education and a degree.

— He is confident and competent without ego.

— He is a "take-charge" guy who is chivalrous and respectful.

— He possesses strength greater than mine and can make decisions for both of us.

— He is a partner. He compliments me and helps me grow.

— He's not afraid to communicate. Willing to be completely honest and talk through things big or small, and once resolved, to not bring them up again.

— He makes me laugh and smile regularly.

— He is fit. Leads a healthy lifestyle.

— He is a role model for my girls and will accept them as his own one day.

— Enjoys sex and wants to make love to me regularly.

— He is financially stable and responsible. He doesn't need me for additional income. He can provide for both of us, but respects my independence and ability to work.

— He is caring and compassionate to me and others alike.

— He is on time or calls to let me know he's running late.

— He is my best friend and understands my "love language."

— He is willing to try new things together. Enjoys alone time as well as time with friends/entertaining.

— He does not have a temper and does not use foul language or call me ugly names.

— He is honest.

— He enjoys meeting new people.

— He promises never to go to bed angry.

— He accepts me for who I am and doesn't want to change me.

Chris' list of attributes he was looking for in his future spouse:

— **Shares my Christian faith and practices it regularly**. As we mentioned in the book, it makes it much more likely that your marriage will be successful if you share the same faith. My faith is important to me, and I wanted someone who I could share that with, talk about it with and attend church regularly with.

— **Beautiful**. As the old saying goes, "Beauty is in the eye of the beholder," and this is true. I knew that it was important for me to be with a woman who was beautiful to me both inside and out. I wanted a woman who, when she walked into a room, took my breath away.

— **Smart**. I knew that I needed to have a woman who could keep up with me mentally. I've written 17 books, hundreds of articles and, of course, read hundreds and hundreds of the same over the years. Intellectual curiosity is important to me, and I wanted a woman who was growing in that way herself.

— **Funny**. I like to laugh, and I like to make people laugh. I wanted a woman who could make me laugh and one who found my sense of humor funny. I told Denise early on that if we got married, I would promise to always make her laugh.

— **Kind**. To me, the heart matters a lot. I wanted a woman who was compassionate and kind. A woman who cared deeply about other people.

— **A good companion who shares many interests with me**. Getting remarried in my later years, I knew that a lot of the success of my second marriage would be about finding the kind of woman I enjoyed sitting on the back porch in the mornings drinking coffee with, or sitting across the table with every night over dinner and being able to carry on a conversation. It would be about finding the woman I could take long road trips with and enjoy. As I like to say it, "Someone I could pal around with."

— **Enjoys a healthy, vigorous and regular sex life**. Sex is different for everyone. There is no right and wrong, just preferences. Some people need sex five to seven times a week, and others can have sex once or twice a week. I knew that I needed to find a woman whose libido matched my own!

Appendix B - 45 Questions and Discussion Starters to Get to Know Spouse Better

1. What is your favorite magazine?

2. What are your favorite books?

3. What is your favorite movie?

4. What's your favorite genre of music?

5. What's your favorite drink?

6. Where is your dream vacation?

7. What's your favorite food?

8. Who's your favorite actor?

9. What would your dream house be like?

10. What songs do you know by heart?

11. If you could have anyone in the world over for dinner, who would it be?

12. Would you like to be famous?

13. What is your greatest accomplishment so far?

14. What is your favorite memory?

15. What is your worst memory?

16. What does friendship mean to you?

17. Who inspires you to be better?

18. What do you want your tombstone to say?

19. Have you ever thought of writing a book? What would it be about?

20. What is something you will never do again?

21. Tell me about an embarrassing moment in your life.

22. If you found a briefcase of money on the street, would you keep it?

23. What's your favorite piece of clothing you own?

24. What is the most annoying habit that other people have?

25. Are you usually early or late?

26. What do you waste too much time on?

27. What age do you wish you could permanently be?

28. What city would you most like to live in?

29. Where is the most relaxing place you've ever been?

30. What does a perfect weekend look like?

31. What's your dream car?

32. What is something that people love but you just don't get the point of?

33. What are you most looking forward to in the next five years?

34. How different was your life one year ago?

35. What's the best way to start the day?

36. What is the luckiest thing that has happened to you?

37. What was the best compliment you've received?

38. What do you spend the most time thinking about?

39. What is your favorite smell?

40. What would you do if you knew you were going to die tomorrow?

41. If you could choose how to die, what way would you die?

42. Who do you know who is living life to the fullest?

43. If you were given an envelope with the time and date of your death inside, would you open it?

44. If you died today, what regrets would you have about your life?

45. What is holding you back from achieving your goals?